Aquinas on the Web?

Aquinas on the Web?

Doing Theology in an Internet Age

Jana Marguerite Bennett

t&t clark

Published by T&T Clark International
A Continuum Imprint

The Tower Building   80 Maiden Lane
11 York Road   Suite 704
London   New York
SE1 7NX   NY 10038

www.continuumbooks.com

New Revised Standard Version Bible: Anglicized Edition, copyright 1989, 1995, Division of Christian Education of the National Council of the Churches of Christ in the United States of America. Used by permission.

British Library Cataloguing-in-Publication Data
A catalogue record for this book is available from the British Library

ISBN: HB: 978-0-567-21065-4
PB: 978-0-567-30474-2

Typeset by Deanta Global Publishing Services, Chennai, India
Printed and bound in India

For my daughters, Lucia and Gabriella

CONTENTS

Introduction

The inspiration for this book comes from two sources. The first was a conference of young Catholic moral theologians in the early 2000s (i.e. graduate students or professors in their first teaching jobs and not yet tenured), named New Wine New Wineskins. At that conference, we discussed what might be some of the generational differences between our work and that of our already tenured colleagues. The internet came up as a possibility, but no one could quite say, at the time, why that would matter.

This book is partly an attempt to answer the question of why the internet matters for doing theology, though at this point, I am now part of the generation gap as compared with my students! There is a generation gap when it comes to technology, but this gap is not generally about "who can use it" versus "who cannot use it." Rather, it's more about "who sponges it up" versus "who necessarily takes a more considered approach about what to include." I think the fact that there is a generation gap is important. I think it's important that there are voices that can both name what the world is like when a technology is simply presumed and be highly reflective about technological use.

The second source is from a discussion board of which I've been a member since the mid-2000s. This was a group of mostly Catholic women, ranging in age from the late teens to the late fifties. Their purpose in gathering, initially (back in 1998), was to find a group of people who could be supportive of the Catholic Church's teachings against contraception. By the time I encountered the group (in the course of figuring out how to "do" a mixed Catholic/Protestant wedding), the membership was still interested in questions about the church's teachings on contraception, but as time went on, I discovered that there was far, far more diversity in discussions that I would have thought at first. The so-called liberal voices – contraceptive using, pro-gay marriage antideath penalty voices – mingled with the so-called conservative voices – homeschooling, noncontraceptive using, libertarian voices. Most times people simply defied categorization.

What made this group particularly interesting, though, was its longevity (still going strong at 14 years), its commitment to praying for each other and the fact that contraception is only a tiny percentage of the conversations that happen there every day. Very often people will raise questions that most moral theologians like me would rather raise in a bar over a beer, but these women wanted to tackle the questions with great intensity. Abortion, homosexuality, divorce, how to raise faithful teenagers, what to make for dinner during Lent – all became important questions.

I realized at some point that I was having theological conversations online with the women at this discussion board, and, to my chagrin, I was actually working harder sometimes to get my points across than I might in the classroom with my students. There is a cartoon that has circulated on the web that features a person working at a computer very late at night, telling the spouse, "I'll come to bed in a minute – I just have to finish proving my point to this person on the internet." The cartoon is funny, but like most humor, has a pretty strong grain of truth.

Partly from those conversations, I began to see that many people were talking theology in a variety of internet media: YouTube, Facebook, dueling blog posts, comments left at blogs, comments left at online denominational sites, Twitter, chat rooms, discussion boards, Wikipedia, and on and on and on. Some were trained theologians like me (many academics have blogs these days, or columns, or online journal articles), but many others were simply very interested lay people of the kind that I'd love to see in my classroom any day of the week. They made me want to think more deeply about what I am calling "internet theology" means for offline theology and offline living. How do these various worlds of which we are a part interplay with and affect each other? So, I began to seek out internet conversations and reflect on them in relation to the work I do as a theologian "in the real world."

The result is this book. In the following chapters, I discuss internet theology by discussing blog posts, YouTube videos, and the like in relation to theological doctrines. I try to show some ways in which the internet is indelibly influencing theological doctrines, both positively and negatively. My main argument is that these different means of doing theology (offline and online) need each other in order to speak rightly about God and the Christian life. At the book's conclusion, I offer some suggestions for practicing theology in a Web 2.0 age, and all of these suggestions come from thinking through theology as done on the internet.

At about the same time that I was earnestly studying Thomas Aquinas in graduate school, I was also discovering that there's a lot of interesting theology done on the internet. My world became an interesting mix of theology from a range of sources and that began to form part of the intuition and basis of this book. This book is not directly about Thomas Aquinas, though I do mention him and his work on occasion. Rather, he and his work, especially in the *Summa Theologica*, become a means for reflecting on internet theology for its continuities and discontinuities with "traditional" offline theology. Using the internet changed my habits to some degree, but it has not erased the fact that I am attracted to certain questions and not to others. So, this is necessarily not an exhaustive theology and I do not at all intend it to be a systematic theology.

As with every book, this one comes with several caveats. The first is that I am a professional theologian, engaging what has sometimes been a rather weird world of internet theology. I am a participant in these theological conversations: this is no sociological study of human interactions around a particular subject matter. This is me, doing theology similar to how I might read and respond to a professional colleague, though of course, many of the people I encounter online are not professional colleagues. Internet theologians are a very mixed bag: the people who discuss theology on the internet are sometimes also professional theologians, or at least trained to do theology by professional theologians. Not every theological conversation is interesting; some are downright silly, and indeed, some readers may wonder why I engage some of the conversations mentioned in this book, at all. Yet it is because I recognize that my own theological habits have been shaped, in part, by these theological conversations, that I want to reflect on them – good, bad, silly, all.

So by "theology" I mean the conversations held about God by someone who raises questions about the God Christians (in particular) worship. Theological conversation is not limited to professionally trained theologians. That means internet theologians are often lay people with little or no training in the traditional university. Rather, they have learned to do theology on the internet, and that is, sometimes, a very different way of doing theology and of raising questions. Professional and lay theologians are jumbled

together in internet theology and I have aimed not only to recognize the
differences in peoples' backgrounds but also to treat seriously
the questions that both academic and nonacademic theologians
raise.

All that said, I am investigating internet theology with the view
of an academic theologian: I therefore see some conversations as
theological and others as not, and that is a limitation of what I am
doing here. I bring my training into the mix to see how questions
raised in internet theology might have a bearing in offline theology,
and vice versa. My academic theological training necessarily butts
heads with the internet medium.

I am decidedly not investigating these conversations from
a sociological point of view, though I do think sociological
investigations of the internet have a place. Just as theologians feel
free to have discussions with long-dead people – Augustine and
Thomas Aquinas – in ways that historians must sometimes feel
frustration with because it seems achronistic, so I am thinking
theologically about discussions that I am sure also raise sociological
questions. However, I am not doing ethnographic studies or surveys
or using any of the other tools that sociologists use so often in their
discourse about theology and the internet.[1]

Another important caveat is the medium itself: it both opens up
and closes up certain kinds of theological inquiry. When I do Google
searches questing after theological discussions, I have necessarily
been linked to some of those conversations but not all; this is not
necessarily my choice but the way the architecture of browsing the
web with Google (or Bing) works. People should be aware of the fact
that the way one accesses the web definitely influences the "choices"
we have in encountering websites, as I discuss at various points in
this book. Eli Pariser has written an excellent book called *The Filter
Bubble: What the Internet is Hiding From You*, and he discusses
that when I do a Google search (of "theology," for example) on my
office computer, I am very likely to get different search results than

---

[1] One of the questions I am sure that sociologists of religion would raise about the
internet and theology is the "insider/outsider" question. That is, the perspective
with which one approaches the conversation; one on the "inside," a practitioner
of the religion (or in this case, of the internet theology) is usually distinct from the
perspective of one on the "outside" who seeks a supposedly objective view of that
religion. See *The Insider/Outsider problem in the Study of Religion: A Reader*, Russell
McCutcheon, ed (London: Cassell, 1999) for a thorough discussion of this problem.

my sister who lives three thousand miles away. Google caters its search engine results toward individual users, which means that a lot of information gets by. One does not necessarily encounter the people one wants to encounter. Pariser discusses how to bypass the filters at his blog. His tips include getting rid of cookies, eliminating web search histories, turning on privacy controls at Facebook, never mentioning your birth year, and the like.[2]

Even though I have aimed to "pop" the filter bubble, I am also aware that even if the filters are not there, I would still not "see" all there is to see on the internet. There is simply quite a lot of stuff there. There are surely a great many theological conversations I have missed – surely better ones than those I discuss in this book. In addition, technologies come and go and it is beyond my ability to make predictions about which of the kinds of Web 2.0 media I mention in this book might or might not still be influential by the time the book is published. Will some things be obsolete? Will my argument make sense? But as the reader will see in the course of this book, I see that the internet is simply part of life; of course it changes, but it also stays remarkably the same in many ways too. The internet – perhaps despite all our best striving to name it as a "new" thing – has been part of the way that Christians continue to pass on and embody Christian traditions. So even if there are changes, I do not think that life will be so entirely divorced from what has come before that these words will make such little sense.

So, doing theology on the internet is a bit like sending a book manuscript off to a publisher's, only to realize that several seminal works have just been published that should, really, have been included in the manuscript just sent out. So, I do this work knowing that I am always merely in the middle of answering the question, never finished. Of course, this is the nature of theology, regardless.

Someone is likely to raise the question: Why write this as a printed book rather than as an online book? My answer is that while I think blogs are excellent ways to have vigorous theological debate, I think the medium of a book enables better comparison and deeper reflection of both offline and online theologies. I think that one of the things the internet age will force us to do is think

---

[2] Eli Pariser, "Ten Ways to Pop Your Filter Bubble," *The Filter Bubble*, (date unknown) http://www.thefilterbubble.com/10-things-you-can-do. Accessed July 19, 2011.

more about how we are saying what we say and to discern more actively which media are the best for thought and action.

Still another caveat: from a academic point of view, I am not a scholar of Thomas Aquinas nor of most of the other theologians who feature in these pages. This is probably evident in the fact that I have raised so impertinent a question as "Aquinas on the web?" I read Thomas, Augustine, John of Damascus, and the like regularly, and in this book, I am indebted to those who do write about them in more scholarly ways. My use of Thomas and other theologians here is meant to be one way to think about theological conversations for how well internet theology is part of the Christian practice known as "doing theology." I use people like Thomas precisely because Thomas does it so well and is so well known.

I am likewise not entirely a scholar of technology, though I do clearly develop a theology of technology of a sort in this book. Albert Borgmann, Sherry Turkle, Manuel Castells, Brian Brock, and many, many others, have become companions for me in this study, but I come to this discussion as an educated academic hoping to be educated further still about the ways in which technology is part of my world. My vantage point as neither a Thomistic scholar nor a scholar of technology enables me to see ways to join the two together, to think about how Thomas Aquinas is, indeed, "on the web."

In addition to all of the scholars to whose work I am indebted, I am also highly grateful to the following colleagues and friends: I am very grateful to several graduate students from the University of Dayton who read, commented on, and helped me edit these chapters; Adam Sheridan, Katherine Schmidt, and Susan Mohall, to name a few. Susan, in particular, read through all of the chapters and did fact-checking and bibliographic work. The following colleagues at both the University of Dayton and Hampden-Sydney College either read versions of these chapters or contributed their helpful thoughts: Brad Kallenberg, Matthew Levering, Kelly Johnson, Dennis Doyle, Vincent Miller, Sandra Yocum, Michael Utzinger, Bob Hall, and Jerry Carney. Brian Brock, Brent Waters, Dana Dillon, Holly Taylor Coolman, Jason Fout, Craig Hovey, and Peter Slade also helpfully commented on one or more chapters. I am grateful to the College Theology Society, the Society of Christian Ethics, New Wine New Wineskins, the Ekklesia Project, and Ashland University for allowing me to present papers and workshops at conferences on this subject, and I am further grateful for a research grant from the University of Dayton Research Institute for the summer of 2011, which allowed me to complete this project. Thomas Kraft has been an amazing editor to work with, and I owe him much for his help in moving this project forward.

And finally, this work could not have been completed without the forbearance and grace of my daughters, Lucia and Gabriella, and my husband, Joel. Thank you.

Feast of Therese of Liseux, 1 October 2011

1

Can Thomas tweet? Theology *about* the internet

Kimberly Hope Belcher, Tweeting the Summa Theologiae? Who would do that? [Oh, yes, I would.]

> **Obj 1:**
> Twitter is inappropriate for any serious endeavor. The ST is a serious endeavor. Therefore, it should not be tweeted.

> **Obj 2:**
> 140 characters are not enough to get any real theology done.

> **Obj 3:**
> People on Twitter are unlikely to appreciate the substance and depth of Thomas Aquinas' great work.

> **Contra:**
> "The Master of Catholic Truth ought not only to teach the proficient, but also to instruct beginners" (ST Prologue). Therefore http://twitter.com/summatheologiae.[1]

---

[1] Kimberly Hope Belcher, "Tweeting the Summa Theologiae," at *PrayTell Blog*, (July 13, 2010) http://www.praytellblog.com/index.php/2010/07/13/tweeting-the-summa-theologiae/. Accessed September 2, 2011.

Thomas Aquinas does happen to be online in some fashion. In addition to the fact that his major work, the *Summa Theologica*, is being tweeted (an internet program that lets people transmit very short, instantaneous statements to those people who choose to "follow" them), he is on Facebook (an internet program that lets people "friend" others, whether they know them or not, and share mundane and also interesting information about their day, photos, and links to websites of interest), blogs (an internet version of a journal, though much more public), and web pages all his own. He has more than one Twitter account. He posts daily quotes, but what is rather more impressive is that he has a 140-character daily tweet his massive *Summa Theologica*.

The next question might well be whether it means anything of significance that Thomas is online and interacting with people via his twenty-first-century stand-ins. When I first started thinking about the way theology is done in an online context, it seemed to me that an apt analogy could be made between the means by which Thomas, in the thirteenth century, carried out his scholastic theology, and the means by which twenty-first-century people practiced theirs. Thomas' disputational method took the form of first, asking a question, then probing the known authorities for their answers to the subject, developing an answer to the question that took those authorities into account (or, alternately, rejected those authorities for some good, stated reason), and then replying to the authorities on why his answer was better.

By comparison, many different kinds of internet conversations facilitate asking and answering theological questions that have some of the characteristics of scholastic disputation. For example, Yahoo! Answers is a website that invites people to ask questions such as: "Is studying Christian theology flawed because the entire subject rests on the belief that the myths are true?"[2] Other internet users answer questions based on their knowledge and expertise. The question asker and other internet users then can read through the answers and make determinations about the best answers, and collectively, they can vote on the best answer. These questions often lead to further questions, again similar to the way disputational theology operated. The open-ended nature of the questions, the

---

[2] Desiree, "Is studying Christian Theology Wrong Because the Entire Subject Rests on the Belief that Myths are True," (2010) http://answers.yahoo.com/question/index;_ylt =At3puprUGp9Puvqua85XQOAjzKIX;_ylv=3?qid=20100422211906AAv9TOJ (2010). Accessed September 2, 2011.

ability to consult a wide range of answers, and the evaluation of answers for their suitability are some of the points of comparison to Thomas' work.

Like most analogies, of course, I found in time that this one fell short. There are ways in which internet theology is very unlike Thomas' disputational method, such as the fact that on the internet, someone might claim to be authoritative about a subject on which they know nothing. The collective voices on the internet do not always do well in their assessment of answers; sometimes an answer is deemed "good" for its "coolness" factor. The amount of reflection that occurs over these answers is dubious by comparison to the thoughtful precision of Thomas' analysis. Thomas' authorities are far less able to be interactive with him than internet theologians tend to be with one another.

Still, theological conversation goes on and on; shouldn't interested people be participating? Indeed, don't Christians have something of a mandate to participate in theological conversations where they happen? The Christian tradition is, after all, comprised of people who care about what we say about God and how we say our words about God (I am thinking here about the many years of heated debate it took to develop the Nicene Creed that is familiar to so many).

Moreover, the theological conversations that happen on the internet have a tendency to spill over to "real life" and affect the theology done offline. Consider, for example, a chance remark that Pope Benedict XVI made on a plane trip in 2009. In an offhand comment made to reporters on his flight, the pope said that AIDS is "a tragedy that cannot be overcome by money alone, that cannot be overcome through the distribution of condoms, which even aggravates the problems."[3] What followed from his remark were days, and in some cases, weeks, of conversation about the pope's comments, theologically and otherwise. The conversation did not chiefly take place among academic theologians, who had previously been seen as the purview for a debate like this, especially on such a hot topic as contraception. Yet, while a few academic theologians did weigh in on the pope's comment, a search among the usual academic databases reveals very little commentary on condoms and AIDS.

---

[3] Riazat Butt, "Pope Claims Condoms Could Make AIDS Crisis Worse," *The Guardian*, (March 17, 2009) http://www.guardian.co.uk/world/2009/mar/17/pope-africa-condoms-aids. Accessed December 21, 2009.

I suspect this is in part because academic theologians, particularly Catholic theologians, think that this is a tired debate (one that has been conducted since at least the promulgation of the 1968 document *Humanae Vitae*, which spells out the Catholic Church's teachings on contraception) that has become rather irrelevant, since most American Catholics use artificial contraception anyway, and the magisterium has effectively prevented much conversation about it.

Rather, the lively conversation and vigorous debate on the Catholic Church's teachings on contraception took place in the midst of a mostly nonacademic audience via Web 2.0 formats. This is not the first time a pope's comment or remarks by other religious leaders has sparked debate in this form. Similar discussions emerge following mainline Protestant votes on homosexuality, for example, or in an evangelical Protestant conversation about Pastor Rob Bell's book on universal salvation (I discuss this further in Chapter 5). In all of these situations, internet theology makes it onto the pages of the so-called secular media like the *New York Times*; the offline world marvels at the questions and intensity of the theological debate happening online.

Theology about the internet: The good, the bad, and the tool

That there is theology done online and that it has some kind of impact on offline theology is indisputable. Still, what is a Christian to do in terms of assessing these theologies? Just because theology is done online doesn't make it right or good or fruitful for Christian life. For example, if we ultimately decided that the internet, as a medium, is evil, it would be rather pointless even to consider the question of whether to do theology there, any more than we could expect, say, reflections on whether murder is a theological act to lead us toward the mystery that is God.[4]

---

[4] Though I note that a determination about the goodness or evilness of murder is itself a theological claim. The distinction I am making is that there is no way, within a paradigm where murder is acceptable, to do theology beyond naming murder as an evil.

There have been several theologians who have raised good questions about the impact of the internet (and technology in general) on Christians' ability to live as witnesses for God. This section discusses some of the key people who reflect *about* the internet. These are people largely reflecting on others' activities, as outsiders, rather than approaching the theology from an insider's vantage point.

Before I turn to reflection about the internet, however, some brief introduction to terminology and the state of the field is in order. One distinction is that between "online" and "offline" communication, or the online world in distinction with the "real world." As Heidi Campbell suggests, "Online is applied to that which takes place in a computer network environment, such as interaction facilitated through the internet. . . . Similarly, the term 'offline' is used to describe any facet of life occurring away from the computer screen."[5] A second difference is the distinctiveness of Web 2.0 from its predecessor Web 1.0. Web 1.0 involved a person and a personal computer; as James van den Heever notes, "the application resides on the personal computer and so does whatever individual users use that application to create. . . However, as the Internet grew and developed its own culture, this paradigm began to change, and value began to move from the personal computer onto the Internet itself."[6] For example, one might consider the difference between websites that simply reiterate print information, and Web 2.0 websites that invite participation. To continue reflection on the Catholic Church, for example, we can consider that the Vatican's website is primarily in Web 1.0 format, with not-very-easily-searchable content that mirrors the print copies of *Lumen Gentium*, *Humanae Vitae*, and the like. Their content was inputted on personal computers by Vatican officials; the appropriate Vatican office has say-so over the content; people can search the information and quote it, but they cannot change the content itself except by hacking the system. In Web 1.0, legal, social, and cultural boundaries are preserved.

---

[5] Heidi Campbell, *Exploring Religious Community Online: We Are One in the Network* (New York: Peter Lang, 2005), xvi.

[6] James van den Heever, "Web 2.0: Technology for the Postmodern Sensibility and its Implications for the Church," *Journal of Theology for Southern Africa*, 132 (November 2008): 86–107, 94.

By contrast, a definition from Wikipedia (of course) pinpoints what is meant by Web 2.0:

> The term **Web 2.0** is associated with web applications that facilitate participatory information sharing, interoperability, user-centered design,[1] and collaboration on the World Wide Web. A Web 2.0 site allows users to interact and collaborate with each other in a social media dialogue as creators (prosumers) of user-generated content in a virtual community, in contrast to websites where users (consumers) are limited to the passive viewing of content that was created for them. Examples of Web 2.0 include social networking sites, blogs, wikis, video-sharing sites, hosted services, web applications, mashups, and folksonomies.[7]

A common suggestion with Web 2.0 sites is that people have now entered a more democratic and freeing environment. In the imagination schooled by Web 2.0, *Humanae vitae* or any other Vatican document is open to user changes so that there is a communal sense of ownership with what is being written and posted. No one exclaims about copyrights, nor is anyone going to worry about whether John Doe *can* say what he just said in the text, because Web 2.0 simply *does* allow for and, more to the point, invites, that kind of interaction.[8]

One of the differences is that the internet has made its users "theologians" of a sort – even those who would not profess Christian beliefs find themselves using theological terms to describe the internet. For example, one technology blogger describes the "rapture" as the moment when there will be super intelligent machines.[9] The internet has also caused Christians to think about theology and write about it, even if they are not clergy or

---

[7] "Web 2.0," http://en.wikipedia.org/wiki/Web_2.0. Accessed May 17, 2011.

[8] I am aware of the current rise and development of Web 3.0 and "cloud computing" using interfaces such as Google Wave. These technologies are still a bit too new to think adequately about their effect, though given that both Web 3.0 and cloud computing have Web 2.0 technologies as their base, I suspect that some of what I say here may well be pertinent for Web 3.0.

[9] Andy Dayton, "The Rapture of the Geeks," at *Being Blog*, (June 4, 2008), Krista Tippett, blog owner, American Public Media, http://blog.onbeing.org/post/37176264/ the-rapture-of-the-geeks-andy-dayton-associate. Accessed May 26, 2011.

professional theologians. As one blogger succinctly describes the Christian blogging world: "We know more than our pastors."[10]

The internet as tool. . .

One prominent way of thinking about the internet is as a communication tool, like the telegraph or radio.[11] On this paradigm, the perception is that the user bears the responsibility of determining how that paper or copy machine can be used (for throwing spitballs? Or for building origami?) because the tool itself is neutral. Those who subscribe to such a view often see that the internet is merely a recapitulation of what happened to theology during the advancement of the printing press. Elizabeth Eisenstein notes of the printing press: "[b]oundaries between priesthood and laity, altar and hearthside, were effectively blurred by placing Bibles and prayerbooks in the hands of every God-fearing householder."[12] So too, in an internet age, technology is blurring boundaries, but in a way that perhaps facilitates transmission of the gospel.

The internet is a medium for communication just like typewritten church bulletins were a medium for communication. Churches put their information "up" on the web because people use search engines to find that information, and some people exclusively so. The diversity of communication styles led, many hoped, to reaching diverse audiences and so drives the hopes of Christian evangelism in the twenty-first century.

The tool view is questioned by people who see that the internet is far more than a simple means of posting information that could otherwise be found in books. This is especially the case in a Web 2.0 world. Sherry Turkle, a psychologist at MIT who has studied the impact of computers, robots, and the internet on humans, writes

---

[10] Tim Bednar, "We Know More than Our Pastors," sites.google.com/site/djchuang2/WeKnowMoreThanOurPastors.pdf. I discuss this article further in Chapter 4.

[11] See, for example, the Pontifical Council for Social Communications, "Ethics in Internet," (February 22, 2002) http://www.vatican.va/roman_curia/pontifical_councils/pccs/documents/rc_pc_pccs_doc_20020228_ethics-internet_en.html, section 2. Accessed October 20, 2010.

[12] Elizabeth Eisenstein, *The Printing Press as an Agent of Change*, 2 vols. (Cambridge: Cambridge University Press, 1980), 425.

against the tool view: "My colleagues often objected, insisting that computers were 'just tools.' But I was certain that the 'just' in that sentence was deceiving. We are shaped by our tools."[13] Naming the internet as a tool makes it seem to be something we can pick up and put down at will, as we would a hammer for constructing something, or a pen for signing a check. We do always have access to these tools in some kind of "Inspector Gadget" kind of way. Web 2.0, however, has perhaps given rise to tools that are often not separate. We can now name a technological class, people who are constantly connected to the internet via their smartphones, and who, moreover, find it exceedingly difficult to disconnect from them, as though their phones were a body part.

The internet as evil?

Some versions of "the internet as tool" recognize that tools are not merely neutral but, in fact, shape us and our ability to respond to the world well. So, some raise the question, "Is the internet a force for good or evil?" Is the internet largely good, or bad, for theology?

The quote at the beginning of this chapter about Thomas tweeting notes some of the reasons why theologians have been concerned about theology done on the internet: for example, that Twitter cannot be substantive or serious enough for thinking about the great Thomas Aquinas' metaphysics and theology. Belcher imagines her interlocutors in this conversation, but the concerns she raises are concerns that underlie many peoples' theological assumptions. In academia, online journals are often seen as lower in quality than offline journals, even if both are peer-reviewed, simply because of the format. Wikipedia is rather famous for professors' derisive remarks, compared with the august, offline, but equally error-prone *Encyclopedia Britannica*.[14]

It is not simply academic quality that has many concerned, though. Theological issues are raised as well. Some theologians name internet technology itself as evil because it seems to be a space

---

[13] Sherry Turkle, *Alone Together: Why We Expect More From Technology and Less From Each Other* (New York: Basic Books, 2011), Introduction. Kindle Edition.

[14] Daniel Terdman, "Study: Wikipedia as Accurate as Britannica," CNET News (December 15, 2005) http://news.cnet.com/2100-1038_3-5997332.html. Accessed September 6, 2011.

where we can be disembodied minds and ignore our bodies. David Kelsey writes about the importance of bodies:

> If coming to understand God involves deep changes in personal bodies, then teaching and learning that aims at deepening understanding of God inherently involves the organic personal bodies of both teachers and learners... Are virtual space and virtual presence adequate media for communication among personal organic bodies, or is 'virtual' just a euphemism for 'bodiless'?[15]

If this is the case, we are guilty of denying the traditional Christian doctrines of creation and incarnation, at the least. Christian theology holds that humans were created with ensouled bodies. If we try to operate without our bodies, we are trying not to be human, and therefore trying to be God. Even more, because Christian belief is that the Father sent the Son to the world so that God would become enfleshed, any attempt to be disembodied is a denial of God's great gift to us in Jesus Christ. This is because humans have bodies and God wanted to be graciously "with us" rather than aloof, and that required a body.

If this view of the internet as disembodied is correct, the problem for Christians is not only that we deny certain crucial doctrines, but also that this disembodied view looks distinctly like a very old set of views that have already been condemned as heretical. These are the views of the "Gnostics." Gnosticism is a term that refers to several groups of people in the second century. Each of these groups had their own distinctive characteristics so that it is difficult to find any one thread that connects them. Nonetheless, in the twenty-first century, people tend to see "Gnostic" as referring universally to the belief that the spirit is good, but the body is bad. Contemporary theologian Christo Lombard uses the term "electronic gnosticism" suggesting that the internet itself is an immaterial medium that does not require physical or material participation and therefore is antithetical to Christianity, which is, after all, very material. For both second-century Gnosticism and electronic Gnosticism, spirit (and soul) is redeemed, but the body is condemned. The problems with Gnosticism are similar to the problems with the internet in

---

[15] David Kelsey, "Spiritual Machines, Personal Bodies, and God: Theological Education and Theological Anthropology," *Teaching Theology and Religion*, 5.1 (2002): 2–9, 9.

that, if one celebrates the idea of being disembodied, then one is also denying both the importance of creation and the incarnation.

For those who see the internet as largely bad, there is a larger problem. Christo Lombard, for example, is not only concerned with the Gnosticism, but also with justice and love. He argues that the internet as a medium "excludes non-Western theologians from using the internet for research" because it requires expensive technology. Even more, Third-World peoples may end up feeling coerced by a world in which they cannot fully participate; colonialism emerges once again, this time in the guise of sleek machinery that promises to "connect us" to a broader world, but in reality disconnects. Thus Lombard fears that the church will no longer hear the cry of the needy if we become too attached to this technology.[16] The electronic Gnosticism of the internet leads directly to poor moral formation and an intense rejection of the gospel.

The internet as good?

By contrast, some theologians have seen the internet as a democratic, open space that enables Christians to share their faith more freely than offline context allows. The Vatican, for example, suggests; "Already, the two-way interactivity of the Internet is blurring the old distinction between those who communicate and those who receive what is communicated, and creating a situation in which, potentially at least, everyone can do both."[17] Moreover, though people tend to see a hierarchical religion as adverse to the kind of two-way dialogue mentioned above, "The Church and the Internet" claims, at least, that a "two-way flow of information" is vital to the being of the church. The internet is salaciously seen as a means for restoring communication between humans but centered on Jesus Christ, as the antithesis to the "pride-driven project of Babel and the collapse into confusion and mutual incomprehension to which it gave rise. . . ."[18]

There is more opportunity for conversation and dialogue, and moreover, with the worshipping church. Some Christians have

---

[16] Christo J. S. Lombard, "Some Ethical Dimensions to Teaching Theology via the Internet," *Journal of Theology for Southern Africa*, 115.01 (March 2003): 43–61, 51.

[17] Pontifical Council for Social Communications, section 6.

[18] Ibid., section 2.

also suggested that there is more opportunity for conversation and dialogue in a Web 2.0 age:

> [S]ome Christians have lately called for a movement of theology out of or at least beyond the academy, primarily into the forum of the Internet. Such sentiments express aims [of]: conversation, not monologue; cross-fertilization of ideas rather than single perspectives; structural openness to other voices and challenging of expertise. As such, these voices have the merit of reminding modern theologians how infrequently they conceive themselves of doing their work within the acoustic realm of the worshiping community, and so become the closed community the bloggers rightly protest."[19]

It is the democratic, freeing, open spaces that provide for dialogue with a broader range of people than one could find in their hometown offline churches, which get cited over and over again in peoples' discussion of the internet as "good" for theology. In her consideration of online religious communities, Heidi Campbell finds that the people she studies name these aspects again and again:"In your own parish and in your own small little world you don't find that many people who are highly literate. This group [the Anglican Communion Online] cares a great deal about theology, their religion, their faith. . . . You don't get to know people in a parish (at this level), so it is much easier to become part of the AC community than it is to become a member of a parish."[20]

> Moreover, several of the people Campbell interviewed claimed that the online religious communities of which they were part enabled them to understand what the church means *theologically*. One person quoted remarked, "[O]nline community . . . is international in scope, so it brings greater immediacy to the 'abstract' doctrine of the universal Body of Christ."[21] Another

---

[19] Brian Brock, *Christian Ethics in a Technological Age* (Grand Rapids: Eerdmans, 2010), 284.

[20] Interview cited in Heidi Campbell, *Exploring Religious Community Online: We are One in the Network* (New York: Peter Lang, 2005), 179.

[21] Interview cited in Campbell, 180.

says, "What I am experiencing on the internet . . . it makes the whole thing of the Bride of Christ more feasible. . . ."[22]

Scripture scholar AKMA Adam, too, finds that the medium of Web 2.0 technology allows for free dispersal of information and social networks, which ultimately makes theological arguments better on his view. Adam became interested in the potential of Web 2.0 via Napster, the online music sharing software developed by Shawn Fanning in 1999. By the end of its first week in existence, it purported about 15,000 users. What interested Adam were the reasons why Napster was so popular, and whether that might relate to how we do theology today. He noticed, for example, that the popularity of Napster was NOT the "cool factor" – Napster was a very simple, rather unattractive design. Napster was, however, free. Adam found that the result of Napster use was that people would eventually buy the CD and go to the concert if they really liked the music. In addition, he found that the more people used Napster, the more they knew and understood music and the more they were able to enter into discussions about the music. Adam found in his study of Napster that users learned how to sift through knowledge and make judgments about what was good on the basis of using the medium more, rather than less.

Adam's theory is that theology does likewise – that it is good to give out theology freely, without worry about interfaces. It is even better to give out theology as much as possible and in as many ways as possible, so that people have more and more access to God's wisdom. His intuition is that thereby people will learn to do theology better, because they have more access to arguments and, more importantly, access to a community that wants to comment on each other's work.[23]

For those who find the internet to be largely positive in theology, it is good precisely because it does something new. The internet brings together peoples and cultures and ideas in ways that truly

---

[22] Interview cited in Campbell, 181.

[23] AKMA Adam, "The Disseminary: What Theological Educators Need to Learn from Napster," http://www.seabury.edu/faculty/akma/Dissem1.html. Accessed January 4, 2010. This link is now broken; Adam's Disseminary still exists at http://disseminary. org.

manifest the global Body of Christ, far better than had been done previously.

The internet as culture

There are still other theologians who remark that seeing the internet as a tool, whether neutral, good, or bad, is a very one-sided way to understand it. The internet is not merely a means of communication, but a whole way of living life. So, theologian Mary Hess suggests, "We all live in digital environments, even theological school faculty. . . we need to keep in mind that digital technologies are cultures in which we are embedded, not just tools that we use."[24] The internet as "culture" suggests that the internet is no tool that can be picked up at will, but is, instead, a community (or communities) of people who are formed and shaped by both the technology and the people who use it. Any parent of a teenager who has despaired of a technological "generation gap" has some sense of the internet as culture. Texting teens have their own language and their own self-understanding that is distinctive from the languages and customs of offline cultures, for example.

As a culture, the internet is both doing something new and also reflecting related offline cultures. That is, the internet becomes a mirror into the way our world works, and thus it becomes intensely complicated. For example, in contemporary culture, community is something Westerners view as a choice, religiously and elsewhere. The internet highlights this aspect of community in terms of both format of a group as well as the focus of a group. Discussion boards and chat rooms might both be named loosely structured "communities." Social networking sites such as Facebook provide further, narrower communities in which theological discussion happens. The idea that the internet is a free space chosen by the individual further supports and enhances peoples' sense that they choose a community and choose to participate in it. What is notable about this space is that while an individual chooses to participate in a community, that does not necessarily make the internet a more

---

[24] Mary E. Hess, "Pedagogy and Theology in Cyberspace," *Teaching Theology and Religion*, 5.1 (2002): 30–8, 37.

dialogical or democratic space when it comes to conversation. When people are choosing the communities to which they belong, and (as in the case of Facebook) delineating the members of their communities, that means that conversation is *less* open rather than more. I am not everyone's friend; I am not part of everyone's community. And, it is other people who are making many of the decisions about whether and how I participate.

In light of this kind of complexity, the theologian cannot simply assess the internet itself as good or bad, but must rather be aware of the ways in which Web 2.0 spaces mediate us. What seems to be democratic and open at first becomes a much more closed society.

Brian Brock is one theologian who takes on the task of naming the complexities of internet technologies. He suggests that we modern humans find ourselves in what he names as a "technological age," in which humans have a vastly different connection to technology than we did in the past. We now presume technology and, most particularly, a progression in our technology use. Our cell phones are now rather ordinary, being supplanted quickly by iPhones and other more interactive phones, and in our imaginations we hope that there will yet be a new and better iteration of what was once a corded dial up phone. In the past, perhaps, technology could be viewed as a set of tools to be taken up and discarded according to how a human being saw fit.

What happens, however, when we no longer have that kind of choice with respect to technology use? Now technology is no mere tool; it is a necessity if one hopes to pass even one course at a university, and it is an expectation in fields of medicine and engineering, as well as the factory. In other words, technology is quite simply the way we exist. One of the effects of this difference is that the technological age exchanges the original ordering of the world for an ordering of our own choosing. We attempt to control a world that we perceive as backward and chaotic, on the way to envisioning an ordered and precise world, made so through our own technological inventions.

The technological age, Brock suggests (following Martin Heidegger and Michel Foucault), therefore cannot help but change our human relationships. We begin to instrumentalize our neighbors and friends, seeing each other as potential means by which we can construct that new world. Brock gives an example of modern warfare: it used to require face-to-face combat, but in a technological age, warfare now becomes automated weapons and high-altitude bombing that allow us to perceive the enemy as a nameless and faceless mass.

What this means is that while there may be an intelligible way to distinguish *when* humans are online and offline (though, as we shall see in the rest of this book, those distinctions are quickly disappearing), there is not an intelligible way to distinguish "now I am seeing the world and using it via technology" and "now I am not."

What also makes considering technology a complex issue for theologians is that technology has a tendency to hide its implications from us. Philosopher Albert Borgmann writes, for example, about the differences between unhomogenized cream and the Cool Whip with which most Americans are now familiar. Cream is lavish, and if we were to trace it to its roots, its origins and make up would be readily apparent to us. Cool whip, however, contains manufactured ingredients mixed together to make something that very closely approximates cream, and which is more readily available than cream. But, moreover, Cool Whip comes with a PR agent and its own advertising to make us believe that it is perfect, fresh, and available, qualities we also wish for ourselves. We too want to be perfect Cool Whip people. And so, says Borgmann, "We remake our personality and appearance to lend them the appeal of availability, we foreshorten our existence into an opaque, if glamorous, surface and replace the depth of tradition and rootedness of life by a concealed and intricate machinery of techniques and therapies."[25]

Borgmann suggests further:

> As long as we overlook the tightly patterned character of technology and believe that we live in a world of endlessly open and rich opportunities, as long as we ignore the definite ways in which we, acting technologically, have worked out the promise of technology and remain vaguely enthralled by that promise, so long simple things and practices will seem burdensome, confining, and drab.[26]

---

[25] Albert Borgmann, *Power Failure: Christianity in the Culture of Technology* (Chicago, IL: Brazos Press, 2003), 17.

[26] Albert Borgmann, *Technology and the Character of Contemporary Life* (Chicago, IL: University of Chicago Press, 1987), 199.

Technology pretends to be new, sleek, and fun, in part because of its PR agents and advertising, and this is the way that it hides its full implications from us. We think that the world of the internet is open and democratic, without seeing that there are ways in which the internet is not so, as I indicated above in my discussion of Brock.

Borgmann suggests that the antidote to this kind of hiddenness is what he names as a "focal practice." "Focal things and practices are the crucial counterforces to technology understood as a form of culture. They contrast with technology without denying it, and they provide a standpoint for a principled and fruitful reform of technology."[27] One example Borgmann gives is that of the meal, which gathers a family that has been scattered to numerous tasks, but is also an occasion for living and forming the way of life of that family. Serving a meal is an act of generosity, says Borgmann, and the food that is served ideally draws us closer to other community members and ultimately makes the world more open and more connected than technology can do. Other focal practices are fishing, or mountain climbing, or the Eucharist.

Theology and the internet as practices

Where, then, do theologians go from here? If seeing the internet as a culture is right (and I think it is), the question still remains on how to assess theology done on the internet. Can the internet provide space for theological conversation such that the theology that comes out of those conversations says anything truthful about God, the church, Christian discipleship, and so on? Theology names the task of saying words about God, but God is always mysterious to humans precisely because we recognize we are not God. In this life, though, it is impossible to plumb the depths of that mystery and to know God. Good theology is therefore always a discussion between humans who seek to understand the mystery that is God more fully.

If that conversation is to be fruitful, however, it does no good if the conversation partners do not clearly share common ground, for instance, the creed. That is, the question about the degree to which Web 2.0 does something "new" is actually a key question, and so part

---

[27] Albert Borgmann, *Power Failure*, 23.

of the aim of this book is to explore how Web 2.0 theology interacts with, shapes, and is shaped by more traditionally done theology (or, what I name throughout this book as "offline theology"). Against those who want to argue that Web 2.0 is offering something entirely new, I claim that Web 2.0 theological discourse only makes sense in the context of theological traditions.[28] Moreover, I will show that Web 2.0 theological conversations articulate the same kinds of concerns and rhetorical uses that noninternet conversations contain. At the same time, as Sherry Turkle suspected, the technology is shaping us as well. People who think theologically (which is, of course, not limited to the so-called academic theologians) need to be aware of the ways in which internet theology shapes the present debates.

I named this book *Aquinas on the Internet?* in part because in the hopes and dreams of its best participants, Web 2.0 in the world of theology seems to take on characteristics of theological debate, perhaps even characteristics of one of theological debate's masters. After all, if Web 2.0 were so thoroughly divorced from theological traditions of the past 2000 years that Christian theologians could not even begin to identify theological conversations there, it would be an immediate conclusion that Web 2.0 spaces do not provide for Christian theological conversation. So a discussion about the possibility of Web 2.0 theology in conjunction with Thomas Aquinas, or other theologians, should not seem odd.

It is Thomas' very practice of theology and his theological rhetoric that most interests me here in relation to online theology. I suggested above that the internet is a culture, which means in part that it shapes certain practices of theology. So it is the case that we can compare the practices of theology, even across the centuries. At least at the outset, there are some intriguing parallels to be made in this comparison. For example, Alasdair MacIntyre suggests, Thomas Aquinas

[develops] the work of dialectical construction systematically, so as to integrate the whole previous history of enquiry, so far as he was aware of it, into his own. His counterposing of authority to

---

[28] For example, Don Compier notes seven characteristics of rhetoric that could easily be said of the internet: that rhetoric is practical, popular, active, contextual, contingent, polemical, and holistic (in the sense of appealing to reason, emotion, aesthetics, etc.). See *What is Rhetorical Theology? Textual Practice and Public Discourse* (Harrisburg, PA: Trinity International Press, 1999), 10–11.

authority was designed to exhibit what in each could withstand dialectical testing from every standpoint so far developed, with the aim of identifying both the limitations of each point of view and what in each could not be impugned by even the most rigorous of such tests. Hence the claim implicitly made by Aquinas against any rival out of the past is that the partiality, one-sidedness, and incoherences of that rival's standpoint will have already been overcome in the unfinished system portrayed in the Summa, while its strengths and successes will have been incorporated and perhaps reinforced.[29]

A preliminary, cursory glance at what Web 2.0 users say about theology suggests some kind of theological continuity with Thomas' own practice of theology. In users' descriptions of Web 2.0, the claims often sound similar to what MacIntyre suggests of Thomas' disputational form, making Web 2.0 seem like an ideal medium and community in which to do theology precisely because of the ways conversation can be initiated on the web.

For example, Christian bloggers describe the Christian blogging communities of which they are part in terms of an open-ended dialectic. A blogger writes, "Bloggers crave interaction and community. We desire to find the 'truth' not as isolated individuals, who get revelations directly from God, instead we believe the truest truth is found collectively."[30] Another blogger writes, "For me it functions as a sounding board as I think about theology, church, etc. I often post questions that I'm thinking through. . . . I don't see blogging as me telling others how to do church or ministry, but rather as a way of learning and forming networks. . . . It is very interactive."[31] Bloggers and users of social networking sites like Facebook particularly experience a dialectical conversation in their entries, some better and some patently worse. Facebook's set up involves people posting small statements about their current thoughts, or linking to articles that are meant to be thought-provoking. Facebook's participants

---

[29] Alasdair MacIntyre, *Whose Justice, Which Rationality* (Notre Dame, IN: University of Notre Dame Press, 1988), 207.

[30] Tim Bednar, "We Know More than Our Pastors: Why Bloggers are the Vanguard of the Participatory Church," (April 6, 2004) http://www.scribd.com/doc/47331/We-Know-More-Than-Our-Pastors. Accessed November 30, 2009, 14.

[31] Darren Rowse, cited in Tim Bednar, "We Know More than Our Pastors," 22.

also have the option of sending longer notes to select friends in an attempt to initiate conversations.

Unlike Thomas' disputational method, this kind of dialectic does not necessarily probe "the whole previous history of enquiry" in the way that Thomas himself did, as he searched through the Church Fathers and Greek philosophers and contemporary scholars for how they addressed the questions he raised. Concerning the situation about the Pope and condoms in Africa, for example, people often turned to the "great minds" they knew about in order to address the question, quoting from the Catechism, from works by John Paul II. However helpful these may be, these hardly represent past enquiry into the subjects. However, the internet does allow for people to access Aristotle and other great minds and texts easily and cheaply, and there are some bloggers in particular who have written lengthy, very carefully-developed theological of various church teachings.[32]

It can also be argued that Web 2.0 technology does allow for and encourage the kind of "dialectical testing of every standpoint so far developed" that MacIntyre depicts in Thomas. The vastness and boundlessness of internet conversation allow for interaction between many quite disparate viewpoints. The way in which Web 2.0 technology is set up permits a variety of viewpoints to be present, as a way of testing theological questions. Tim Bednar, one of the proponents of this emerging "cyberchurch," writes that the "bazaar of the blogging cyberchurch is naturally susceptible to excesses, untruths, syncretism or blatant heresy. It is not a homogeneous, well-ordered or accurately labeled universe."[33]

Note that it is the theological community in conjunction with the technology of Web 2.0 that enables Adam, Bednar, and others to argue that something good is happening theologically on the internet, and that reflects something of the theological conversation Thomas and other scholastics were able to carry out because of their use of the disputational form. For example, Thomas and his contemporaries learned to do theology by writing commentaries on

---

[32] See, for example, Eric Williams' several posts on the history of the Catholic Church's teachings against contraception, where he focuses on the question of whether natural family planning really looks distinctive from the so-called artificial contraception. "Investigating NFP: Preface" (no date) at http://alesrarus.funkydung.com/archives/2211. Accessed September 30, 2011.

[33] Bednar, 22.

Peter Lombard's *Sentences* on Scripture. Additionally, the monastic and apprenticeship-like formation of young theologians provided communities of spiritually serious people concerned to check each others' work.

Bednar also notes that "bloggers take their faith seriously and actively engage in the process of spiritual formation. This naturally causes them to protect what they believe to be true about the church, faith, praxis and the Bible. . . . In the process, the stories of truth seem to gather strength and eventually overshadow stories of untruth. This is not accomplished through elimination of minority voices; there is no Darwinian 'survival of the fittest' at work."[34] Bednar notes that these are serious, thoughtful people. After all, he says, blogging is a discipline much like prayer is a discipline. They have a stake in maintaining the theological community of which they are part.

As a final note, there is a similarity between MacIntyre's view of Thomas' disputational style as an unfinished system, and the internet's own unfinished system. The scholastic disputational method held sway in part because it had beauty – it was able to bear the weight of the mystery of God precisely because it was unfinished, boundless, open to constant revision and interpretation, since the assumption was that they, like we, are mere humans who cannot fully plumb the depths of who God is. Web 2.0 bears some marks of this kind of scholastic way of thinking because it has its own boundless, infinite form that gives rise to further questions and further delving into its many mysteries. There is seemingly no end to the number of web pages that can be developed for the internet – but even Thomas' *Summa* had to end at some point. For the scholastics, the disputation was a useful tool for understanding God to a greater degree; in this sense those theologians who view the internet as a tool for doing theology seem correct for thinking that using the internet can indeed lead to greater understanding of God by providing answers and even more questions.

To sum up, it seems that Web 2.0 should be a theologian's dream. Some academic theologians have perhaps lamented that our students do not seem to care about doing theology anymore, do not see the beauty of the questions, when in fact, perhaps this developing community of Web 2.0 theologians has been rising to

---

[34] Bednar, 23.

the occasion. Theologians who do not participate in any form of Web 2.0 technology are therefore missing out on an important theological conversation.

The caveat. . .

This preliminary and rather cursory examination of Thomas in relation to some Web 2.0 users' discussions of what they see themselves doing suggests some possibilities for this book's discussion. All this comparison is only at surface level, however. As Brian Brock notes, "What we must ask is whether Internet theology can in fact generate the community of discernment these authors seek."[35]

To assess theology on the web and think critically about the theological culture Web 2.0 spaces engender, we need to focus intently on the theological rhetoric that people use online. To focus on theological rhetoric, though, means more than simply focusing on words; the words always already imply the kind of community to which a person belongs. Consider, for example, what we do when we speak theologically. I often tell my students that theology is words (*logos*) about God (*theos*) and that in the process of making words about God, we realize that those words, which mere humans are speaking and using after all, are ultimately inadequate for expressing the utter mystery of God.

Therefore, our words about God end up being conversations with each other about the possibilities and impossibilities of what could be meant by "God," and in the case of Christianity, such conversations often turn into heated arguments. But arguments about words are themselves *practices* that Christians have as part of their life together. Indeed, I think it would be impossible to think of Christian life without the practice of arguing. (Whether we learn to argue well is another question entirely!) Theologian David Cunningham suggests that there is not generally a recognition of the fact that theology involves argument:

despite the obviously confrontational posture of much Christian theological discourse, few of its practitioners have been willing

---

to admit that it is, in fact, composed of arguments. After all, the word argument implies at least two possible positions; this, in turn, implies multiplicity and contingency, for if argument is possible, then everything could be otherwise. To many observers, such contingency seems alien to Christianity, which often makes quite absolute claims that seem not to admit of alternatives – in turn suggesting little room for argument. And indeed, many theologians attempt to disguise the inherently argumentative character of their claims precisely in order to make them more effective as arguments.[36]

But strangely enough, the community of believers that follows Christ has always been engaged in arguments of some kind or other. The New Testament Christians argued long and hard over whether Christians needed to be circumcised, even if they were not Jewish and about whether meat offered to pagan idols could be eaten. Arguments have changed over the centuries, but that arguments are part of Christian life together. At our best, we argue because we seek to follow Jesus Christ well, and because of that desire to follow Jesus, we worry over whether we, or our brothers and sisters, follow Christ well. How to follow Jesus is worthy of argument. Otherwise, if the ways in which we live our lives together does not matter, we should never have arguments, but this would be a false kind of peace. A "peace" that is kept by allowing anything to be permissible merely suggests (rightly) to outsiders and to Christians both that we do not care enough Jesus' claim on our lives for what we say and do to mean anything. And then, why bother with belief in Jesus at all? There are plenty of other good groups to belong to, and far more fun things to keep myself occupied.

So, in examining the language that internet theologians use with each other, I am also examining the Christian practice of argument, along with other ways that Christian life is practiced and lived online and offline. This is because language implies a certain way of life. If the internet is a culture – and its theology is a subset of that culture – one of the ways to examine it is in its language.

Consider an offline, nontheological example in order to see how language and culture and life relate. Think about the ways in which

---

[36] David S. Cunningham, *Faithful Persuasion: In Aid of a Rhetoric of Christian Theology* (Notre Dame, IN; London: University of Notre Dame Press, 1990), xiv.

language "speaks" a newly minted college graduate who is now off to medical school. The newly minted college graduate converses at or only slightly above a lay person's general knowledge of medicine. While there are some similarities between her undergraduate work and the course work she engages in at the graduate level, and some similarities with what she has heard offhand at her own doctor's appointments, she will also find that if she is to succeed in medical school, she must more avidly learn new language terms and thereby develop a new way of being and thinking. She will learn to think about the human body in Latin terms; she will also thus become adapted to a particularly "medical" way of thinking about the human body as she learns to use those Latin phrases. As she progresses through medical school and begins her series of observations, she will find that this is even more so. She becomes familiar with terms that tend to confound lay people, such as "pediatric oncology," and she learns to rattle off hurried medical abbreviations, to go along with the hurry that is contemporary medical life. Her manner of talking (quickly and with acronyms) implies her pace of life and the kind of change she has undergone, and as she enters further into the field, into doing residency and becoming part of a practice, she will discover that she now has to be at ease in two distinctive "languages": one for the lay people she treats; the other for the medical personnel she will meet.

Christianity, too, is full of its own new word usages and its own way of life. A celebration of the Eucharist, and all the prayer language that goes with it, makes little sense to an outsider. Converting to Christianity, or even converting within Christianity from, say, Presbyterianism to Catholicism, requires learning to use words – even words that are apparently the same – in different ways. Catholics say the "Our Father"; Presbyterians, the "Lord's Prayer" and they say those prayers in different ways which imply certain aspects of culture. For one thing, Presbyterians say, "Forgive us our debts as we forgive our debtors," but Catholics "Forgive us our trespasses as we forgive those who trespass against us." The distinction relates to the history of each people, as they struggled to translate Greek words into English. Also, Presbyterians will proceed right through the Lord's Prayer to the conclusion: "For thine is the kingdom, and the glory, and the power forever." This phrase is included in Matthew 6:13, one of the places where we find the Lord's Prayer in the Bible (though it should be said that there is some question about whether Matthew originally included this phrase; some Christian churches omit this line for being unbiblical because it is not in certain Greek manuscripts.)

In the Sunday Mass, Catholics, however, will stop at the line "Lead us not into temptation but deliver us from evil." They will wait for the priest to say the words, "Deliver us, Lord, we pray, from every evil, graciously grant peace in our days, that, by the help of your mercy, we may be always free from sin and safe from all distress, as we await the blessed hope and the coming of our Saviour, Jesus Christ." Only then, will Catholics progress to the final line of the prayer. Such differences may seem arbitrary at first glance, especially to those for whom language just "is." But consider that the Catholic "Our Father" reflects a certain kind of relationship with a hierarchical priesthood and a tradition that has been handed down from centuries, while the Presbyterian Lord's Prayer reflects a sensibility about adhering to what is in scripture alone.

In this simple example, one can see particular theological conversations, those that are part of the Presbyterian/Catholic traditions, and not only in the rhetoric of those arguments, but also in the way of life that the language implies. The fact that there exists a whole "way of life" then also implies ethics, and considerations about what is the good thing to do, the right "way" of living life in Jesus Christ.

Thus, in this book I seek not to do a theology *about* the internet, but rather, by going to some of the many Web 2.0 spaces (like Twitter and Facebook and blogs), I aim to examine theology *on* the internet. I want to examine theological practice online in relation to internet culture, because I think that theology done on the internet must therefore be assessed for how well it engenders and sustains a Christian way of life. This evaluation can examine the way of life embedded in internet spaces themselves (for example, the various groups professing to meet as churches online) as well as the way of life fostered (or not) in "real life" communities. What I suggest is that if the technology is doing something distinctive, but still rooted in tradition, I can examine theological conversations for the extent to which the internet allows for and participates reciprocally in theological conversation, even and *especially* theological conversations that happened centuries ago.

Accordingly, the rest of this book is set up so as to discuss specific doctrines that Christian theologians have identified over the centuries, such as theological anthropology, ecclesiology, and ethics. A doctrine-specific conversation allows me to focus on the ways in which the internet does and does not participate in and contribute to Christian traditions' theological conversations, and the ways in which a Christian life is or is not affected. Of course, given that part of the effect of an open-ended debate like Thomas' is that doctrine might be developed at any point in the conversation, I will assess whether the strands of theological conversation I find on the internet may represent a development of doctrine rather than a deviation from traditional theology.

In this book, I cannot evaluate every possible doctrine nor do I think it is feasible to write some kind of new internet-related *Summa*. What I have tried to do is examine those doctrines that seem most related to the theological questions people already ask about the internet. Other doctrines may appear as sidelines in my investigations, however.

Chapter 2 therefore investigates the doctrine of God by discussing the claim that the internet focuses on images rather than words. Theologians see a focus on images as a problem because it ostensibly leads people away from the Word known through scripture and toward the dark road of idolatrous thoughts about God. In this chapter I take up some online theological arguments that claim, on the contrary, that it is offline theology that is idolatrous. I then use the work of eighth-century theologian John of Damascus to discuss the problem of images, idolatry, beauty, and form in relation to God, ultimately concluding that the internet need not be idolatrous, and that offline theologians might benefit from the work done by theological discussions online.

Chapter 3 addresses the doctrine of theological anthropology by thinking through one of the central debates about the internet: whether it builds human community or destroys it. On the one hand are those who see that the internet promotes global connections and greater diversity of conversation; on the other hand are those who see that internet use disconnects one from those who are unable to access the internet (people who are economically disadvantaged, who often come from non-Western nations). Additionally, there are questions about gender, race, and disability in relation to the internet. Into all of these questions comes the extent to which technology changes what it means to be human. I discuss the rise of the "social cyborg" and then look back at the questions raised about globalism, gender, and so on, to think about how "theological cyborgology" changes our theological landscape.

Chapter 4 takes up the question of theological authority. In this chapter, I reflect on the extent to which the internet is truly a broadly democratic freeing space, open to a range of ideas that supposedly allows for better and broader conversation, in contrast to the authoritarian views many Christians hold about their church institutions. As I show, however, there are "authorities" online that demonstrate less of a democratic space than internet users suppose. These operations of authority prevent people from fully engaging theological conversation, thus truncating the supposed benefits of this democratic space. But recognizing this fact opens up another theological view of the internet, which is to see Web 2.0 as one of the Powers mentioned in the New Testament. After discussing the internet as a Power, I suggest how Christians might re-envision their use of the internet.

Christians cannot use the internet fruitfully, however, without communities that help shape and form them. Accordingly, Chapter 5 considers whether "church" can exist online. One of the central discussions in this chapter focuses on some top Christian leaders' call for more web participation in order to evangelize, because they see the internet as the next new frontier. Yet I also show how, for internet theologians, there is a consistent concern for "community" which does not neatly fall in line with "the next new thing." What it means to be church for online Christians means being indelibly tied to offline Christian communities as well.

Chapter 6 builds on previous chapters to discuss the shape of Christian moral formation online. In this chapter, I discuss a recent online theological debate about Rob Bell's book *Love Wins*. Bell's book came under fire for raising the possibility of universal salvation. I do not jump into the salvation debate in this chapter, but use it to think about the ways Christians treat each other online, as a means for thinking about ethics, virtuous living, and why we have rules. Against theologians who find the internet to be lacking in promoting the kind of habits that form Christians well, this chapter argues that Web 2.0 technology can, indeed, foster virtuous living.

Finally, I conclude with brief thoughts on how theologians need to respond to Web 2.0. The book as a whole neither wholly embraces Web 2.0, nor rejects it, but instead seeks where the most fruitful ground for Christians might be. In particular, this last chapter returns again to the theme of this chapter: the idea that theology is a practice. But in the conclusion, having discussed and examined the ways of life and practices of online theology, I shall be better able to conclude this book by offering ways that theologians might better live their lives so as to be more faithful theologians, online *and* offline.

2

Idolatry: On whether the internet is a creature created by God

Susan Wise Bauer, writing in her blog "The Well-Trained Mind"

If a digital apocalypse weakens the Christian faith, it means that our hope is not in fact in God, and his power to work in the world; but rather our hope is in the book . . . . As people of God, in an age of speedy instant[an]eous communication and overwhelming information, how do we think about images and words? As creations which need to be redeemed.[1]

Nathan, commenter on "Disappearing Words"

I think I agree insofar as you talk about the "written word" – that is, words understood as visual symbols – but

---

[1] Susan Wise Bauer, "Disappearing Words, Part IV: What do we do about it?" *The Well-Trained Mind: Classical Education for the Next Generation*, (May 11, 2011) http://www.welltrainedmind.com/reflections-on-education/disappearing-words-part-iv-what-do-we-do-about-it/. Accessed June 13, 2011.

> not words in general. In one sense, I think we can definitely say that words are creations. But in another sense, is speaking words really "creating" – or is it only possible to conceive this as a way of thinking after the advent of writing?[2]

The internet conversation:
Is God online?

How are we to find God or think about God on the internet? Peoples' kneejerk reaction to the question, "God on the internet?" is to maintain that, like everything, God is involved, but only at a distance. That is to say, people are rather comfortable about speaking of the internet as a human-made tool; like other tools, it coexists with us humans. Thinking about God on the internet or God in relation to the internet seems idolatrous, though. Similarly, Jesus saves people, but the internet is not in need of salvation (so it seems) in the way that people are in need of salvation. So, the internet becomes a place where people ask questions *about* God to other like-minded people, as evidenced in the many discussion boards and online churches – but the possibility of God on the internet, or God in the internet, becomes almost a taboo subject. At best, inability to have a conversation prevents seeing possibilities about God's interaction online; at worst, it prevents seeing where versions of "god" online are idolatrous.

Thus, while I think there are many theological conversations that carry out (to some extent) online conversations *about* God, what I think is more important are those conversations that raise questions about God *on* the internet. First is the question of whether and how God interacts with us via our human-made tools (if, indeed, the internet can be called a mere tool, a discussion I take up to some degree in this chapter). Second is the question of idolatry: of knowing whether the "god" we see, or don't see, on the web, is the God of Abraham, Isaac, and Jacob, the Triune God Christians worship.

---

[2] Nathan, comment at "Disappearing Words, Part IV: What do we do about it?" *The Disappearing Mind: Classical Education for the Next Generation*, (May 11, 2011) http://www.welltrainedmind.com/reflections-on-education/disappearing-words-part-iv-what-do-we-do-about-it/. Accessed June 13, 2011.

In this chapter, I discuss some of the ways internet theologians have raised and responded to these questions about idolatry, focusing especially on beauty and truth, as two important concepts that arise particularly from considering God and the internet. I conclude by discussing how the internet is a creature, like we are, like the animals are, like even time and history are. Only when can we see that we are creatures among creatures can we put the internet properly in its place as a medium for doing theology.

There are a few internet theologians who point to other possibilities besides the kneejerk reaction of presuming that one's relationship with God simply carries over to the internet. Susan Wise Bauer's discussion of communication at her blog intriguingly suggests that (at least some) offline discussions of God fail to recognize God *because* they have been offline. More importantly, God becomes an idol in the hands of offline people concerned about the effects of "online communication" for one of the central activities of Christianity: reading the Bible. In this particular blog post, Bauer (who is a well-known homeschooling advocate and has an MDiv, as well as a PhD in American Studies, with a focus on American religion) is responding to those who fear a future when people no longer read, particularly a time when scripture is no longer read. They fear a "digital apocalypse" of a kind that will fail to enable people to hear and respond to God's word.

Bauer develops her argument over four distinct blog posts, each of which has numerous comments attached. In the first, she raises the concern: the book is dying (according to numerous authors) and the panic is that this must, somehow, have an effect on Protestant Christians especially, because of their focus on scripture. The shift from print to digital culture is similar to the shift from oral to print culture, say many, except that the shift to print was good, while the current shift is "a very, very, bad thing indeed, because it will make us a violent, distracted, ignorant people, easily manipulated, drowning in trivialities and susceptible to totalitarianism."[3]

In Part II, Bauer discusses why she thinks people are concerned about the digital revolution. Among other reasons, she names:

---

[3] Susan Wise Bauer, "Disappearing Words, Part I" *The Well-Trained Mind: Classical Education for the Next Generation*, (May 5, 2011) http://www.welltrainedmind.com/reflections-on-education/disappearing-words-part-i-the-bad-news/. Accessed June 30, 2011.

We will not be able to concentrate for long periods of time because our attention spans will adapt to screen-sized bits of information.

We will not be able to think logically and sequentially because we'll be so accustomed to processing multiple bits of information simultaneously in all directions.[4]

These concerns, she notes, point to a decrease in left-brain thinking and an increase in right-brain thinking. This is worrisome because our culture, and American Protestant Christianity in particular, is grounded in left-brain logical thinking; moreover, Christians are people of words. Alluding to Doug Groothius, among others, Bauer suggests that humans see this as a problem because

Our faith is grounded in the written word of God.

We are losing the ability to comprehend the written word as well as we used to.

If we cannot comprehend the written word, we will not be able to comprehend God's word.

Our faith will have no grounding.[5]

Thereby, the words by which Christian faith is transmitted will be lost. Such an assertion also presumes that God chose to transmit via words, which are superior, rather than images, which are prone to being deceptive.

Commenters for both the first and second parts find themselves largely wanting to make tongue-in-cheek statements. WildIris says, "I read what you wrote. My attention stayed on task long enough to get to the last sentence, I think." Brian Wasko writes, "I am unable to understand all these words. Could you just do a video or an infographic, please?" But WildIris also reflects, more seriously, on the particular problem of the way the digital age seems to be forming peoples' habits, and thus agrees with what Bauer suggests. "Take a look at the last remaining newspapers and magazines that once

---

[4] Susan Wise Bauer, "Disappearing Words, Part II: What Exactly Are We Worried About?" *The Well-Trained Mind: Classical Education for the Next Generation*, (May 6, 2011) http://www.welltrainedmind.com/reflections-on-education/disappearing-words-part-ii-what-exactly-are-we-worried-about/. Accessed June 30, 2011.

[5] Ibid.

boasted dense pages of print several decades ago. Time Magazine is now reduced to sound bite sized articles and The New Yorker has thinned with age but it still publishes articles of length. . . .I do think the digital age does a good job of pruning ones ability to concentrate, and it seem obsessively addictive, plus it robs one of the capacity to reflect. There is simply too much noise to think."[6]

The third blog post does a deeper analysis of the problem, by investigating Marshall McLuhan's statement, "The medium is the message." Bauer looks at all the media changes that have happened since any of the scriptures were written: tablets to papyrus, papyrus to codex, codex to printed book, and now printed book to digital media. In addition to these changes, however, there is also the question of translation of the words. And so Bauer makes the following critique of McLuhan:

> If the medium is the message, the message of the Word of God is inaccessible to us already. Long before the Internet, the medium had already drastically changed from its original form–so drastically that the message of the Word was lost.[7]

Bauer notes that part of the fear of moving to an image-based culture is that the Ten Commandments prohibit "making idols," and quotes people like Phillip Ryken, Neil Postman, and Arthur Hunt, all of whom conclude that images distract us from God, that "paganism is always image-centered, but that Christianity always prioritizes word." Yet, Bauer says, the Ten Commandments also prohibit using words unwisely: "Do not take the Lord's name in vain." So suggests Bauer,

> And that's the central problem with using the Ten Command-ments to conclude that God likes words and dislikes images: you have to ignore a good bit of the historical and social context of the commands. The Israelites were not to make images of God because that's what they'd always done before. Those images

---

[6] Ibid., [sic].

[7] Susan Wise Bauer, "III. Wrong Assumptions," *The Well-Trained Mind: Classical Education for the Next Generation*, (May 8, 2011) http://www.welltrainedmind. com/reflections-on-education/disappearing-words-part-ii-what-exactly-are-we-worried-about/. Accessed June 30, 2011.

would encourage them to think of God as a bigger and more useful version of the gods they already knew.[8]

By this point, the conversation has hit a nerve. The comments shift from being tongue-in-cheek to some more eye-opening questions, most about the nature of images and their relationship with faith, truth, and beauty. Theron Mathis says, "As an Orthodox Christian immersed in imagery, this provides an interesting argument for the ability of images to communicate truth." Tim writes, "I'm a watercolorist and a Christian. Having been raised a fundamentalist Protestant, I sometimes worry that I am Eve, deceived by the beauty of the garden."[9] Bauer's commenters start to wonder about the materiality they encounter on the internet; they start to buy into the view that the internet, with its images, is profoundly material.

In her final post, having argued against McLuhan's often-quoted statement, "The medium is the message," Bauer discusses why Christians need not worry about the shift from print to digital media. She notes connections between the view some have of the digital age with the view people held of the middle ages:

> Middle Ages: no one reads; incivility and irrationality; Christianity fades. Renaissance; people start reading, civility and reason spread; Christianity returns. This is nonsense. To start with, it equates New Testament Christianity with Reformation Christianity, which I think we should not do. But more seriously, it takes the "improving health" of a society, its absence of superstition, and its rules of decorum as proof that Christianity is gaining power.[10]

Class, and civility, seems equated with Christianity; the Age of Reason seems particularly suited to Christianity, on this view. Bauer does not quite make this connection, but at the heart of Bauer's argument seems to be that the internet tampers with an Enlightenment version of affairs, a version that she ultimately claims is idolatrous. But it is the internet, with its penchant for images and short written messages that is helping Christians see their idolatry.

---

[8] Ibid.

[9] Ibid.

[10] Susan Wise Bauer, http://www.welltrainedmind.com/reflections-on-education/disappearing-words-part-iv-what-do-we-do-about-it/.

Materiality becomes one of the questions for Bauer's commenter "Nathan," who wonders about the differences between words as written and words as spoken. He says, "I think of how key 'hearing' the word is: Paul writing in Romans 10:17 that faith comes through the hearing of the Word. . . ." What about the fact that the Word of God creates us, he asks? Isn't it the Word that gives rise to who we are, rather than the other way around, that words are creatures too? There is something distinctive, he thinks, between written and spoken words.

Bauer's response hits home. She recognizes both the false eschatology in those fears and also the idolatry that lies in the midst of, and as the cause of those fears. A person who really fears a "digital apocalypse" is a person who worships books. God's relationship with us cannot really change though God may find new ways of communicating God's self to us humans.

Bauer's very well-thought out views of the internet show her to be thinking of the web as profoundly material. This is in marked contrast to those who see the internet as profoundly immaterial, perhaps even to the point that another internet user, Frank Den, argues (though with far less finesse and thoughtfulness). In his Web 2.0 collaborative book project, Den suggests that God's relationship with us, and indeed God's very self is changed because the internet entirely sheds new light on who God is. In his project (and blog of the same name), called "The Internet is God," he suggests that the internet is a metaphor for God's nature and appeals to many different religions, and he wants the internet to become an overarching metaphor that is ultimately able to help people cultivate peace and goodwill toward each other. He says,

My contention here is that The Internet throws light on what we call God in all sorts of ways. This does not assume the existence of God; the idea of The Internet as God may help us to approach ideas and ideals that could be called God; whether or not God is a figment of our imagination![11]

One of Den's main points is that the internet is boundless, formless, and unfathomable, much as God is, so that what he sees as

---

[11] Frank Den, "Introduction," *The Internet is God*, (November 25, 2008) http://www.theinternetisgod.org/book/internet-god/introduction. Accessed March 1, 2011.

both absolute and relative positions about God are possible.[12] A commentator at his blog largely agrees, though he misses Den's point about the possibility of something relative also being absolute: "How we see God depends on where we are standing. If we are standing on either side of him and take pictures, he obviously looks different in our pictures. Expecting to come at an image of God which is absolute and looks the same to everyone, is foolish. Nothing in the universe is the same to everyone."[13] The internet therefore enables people to understand God better, perhaps exactly because our speaking about the internet is generally metaphorical.

Like Bauer, but for different reasons, Den suggests that thereby the internet displaces idolatry:

> Another characteristic of the computer is that it is relatively idolatry free, unlike many churches and cathedrals. To the Internet searcher after God, the screen and browser is less important than the experience. It does not matter whether we connect with an Apple, PC or mobile phone, a two inch, 14 inch or 19 inch screen.[14] Den describes idolatry as making material items the most important things in one's life; the internet, though, with its apparent immateriality becomes an apt means to discuss God, who is also, on his account, utterly immaterial.

As we saw in his above quote, his argument does not depend on the actual existence of God. Given his sense about idolatry as physical, this makes sense. An argument that requires the existence of God tends to be based in material evidence. Note, for example, that most of Thomas Aquinas' famous Five Ways revolve around physicality and the senses: we observe that something in motion must have been put in motion by another; we observe that some things are more good and some less good, and the like.[15] Philosophers have often critiqued Thomas for his Five Ways; in a sense, Den continues that

---

[12] Den, "The Nature of God," *The Internet is God*, (November 25, 2008) http://www. theinternetisgod.org/book/internet-god/nature-god. Accessed June 15, 2011.

[13] Vimoh, comment, (December 17, 2009) http://www.frankden.com/2009/12/15/ atheism-and-absolute-truth/#comments. Accessed June 24, 2011.

[14] Den, "Worshipping God," *The Internet is God*, (November 25, 2008) http://www. theinternetisgod.org/book/internet-god/worshipping-god. Accessed June 15, 2011.

[15] Summa Theologica I. 2. 3

kind of critique based in the senses, but now with the internet as an example of a more apt metaphor for thinking about God.

Bauer does not think that the internet will not itself invite idolatry, only that the digital age shows us some of the idolatries we have been engaged with offline. Den, by contrast, fully believes that the internet is a haven from idolatry. With both, it is the fact that the internet plays at all in the conversation – or that it can have something to tell offline theology about sin, idolatry, and the nature of God, that is interesting, and perhaps for some, impudent. Bauer sums up this idea:

> The digital age has made us aware of something which perhaps we were not aware before. And this danger is not the disappearance of words. This danger is the idolatry of words. On the flip side of imagophobia is grammatolatry: the giving over to the medium the power that rests in the message. Worshipping the words rather than the Word-giver, the creation rather than the created; there is also something about that in the Ten Commandments.[16]

Our human "Gods" and the internet

Offline conversation often worries about the internet and idolatry precisely because web-based interaction seems immaterial (along similar lines as the Gnostic complaint from the first chapter) and leads to a vacuum – to be filled by humans rather than by God. Travis Pickell reflects, in a tone strikingly similar to Bauer's though with a decidedly different conclusion: "being too quick to employ new technologies may lead to the divine message being shaped or even substituted by a human medium."[17] So therefore we worship ourselves and our fancy technologies (and worshipping our technology is really only a way of worshipping ourselves) rather than God.

---

[16] Susan Wise Bauer, ibid.

[17] Jean Nicolas Bazin and Jérôme Cottin, *Virtual Christianity: Potential and Challenge for the Churches* (Geneva: WCC Publications, 2004), 2, cited in Travis Pickell, "Thou Hast Given Me a Body: Theological Anthropology and the Virtual Church," *Princeton Theological Review* (Winter 2010): 67–79, 68. Available online at http://www.princetontheologicalreview.org/issues_pdf/43.pdf.

Shane Hipps likewise discusses the ways in which internet media shape our views of the world and ourselves. We can offer fake identities and fake photos, for example, that convey supposedly better images about who we are. Or note the ways that we can manipulate images to make better, buffer, thinner, bustier, images of ourselves – who we wish to be rather than who we are. So we make "graven" images of ourselves, on Hipps' view, images that we desire over truth, goodness, and other transcendental attributes that might lead us toward God in traditional theological thinking.[18] Hipps argues exactly the opposite as Bauer: for God, the medium is, indeed, the message. McLuhan was correct, for God sent Jesus Christ the Word to be the medium and the message. Furthermore, the church, as God's body of witnesses, is the medium and the message God conveys to the world.[19] What that means is that Christians are to be embodied witnesses: "The church exists to embody and proclaim the good news of God's kingdom. If the medium is the message, the message of the gospel is conveyed by the medium of the church's life in the world."[20]

Theologian Graham Ward shares concerns about idolatry, the internet, and embodiment with Hipps, but with greater focus on how internet idolatry links to our modern and postmodern sensibilities. He suggests:

Technology not only delivers the ideal; it mediates the timeless and universal Ideal. Yet it fosters forms of virtual living that are now detached from the Good and from its codependents: the True, the Beautiful, and the Just. As such, virtual living cannot guarantee virtuous development – those moral capacities that come with participation in the Good, the True, the Beautiful and the Just.[21]

The internet merely represents, on Ward's view, an endless desire for the True and the Beautiful (via commercialization of such ideals) so that users of the internet cannot participate in Truth and Beauty themselves but only yearn for it. Thus he writes,

---

[18] Shane Hipps, *Flickering Pixels* (Grand Rapids: Zondervan Press, 2009), Chapter 9.

[19] Hipps, Chapters 16 and 17.

[20] Hipps, 168.

[21] Graham Ward, "Between Virtue and Virtuality," *Theology Today*, 59.1 (April 2002): 55–70, 65.

Cyberspace renders modernity's concern to make knowledge conform to its object so that truth is determined by the adequacy of knowledge to the one reality 'out there', redundant. The knowledge is already pre-packaged and comes complete with a date of manufacture (or updating) and a breakdown of its components. . . .[22]

We no longer have to seek knowledge and truth; they are, apparently, readily available to us in a variety of convenient interfaces that can be bought. We cannot see distinctions between ourselves and God when "attaining knowledge" has been truncated to the phrase "Let me just google that. . . ."

Moreover, Graham argues that the internet fits very well with our postmodern world of questioning categories and foundations of thought,[23] because the internet itself lacks boundaries and sharp distinctions. The internet "makes virtuality" a reality. Because the internet is space that is largely imagined, reality becomes meaningless. This meaninglessness, on Ward's view, tends easily toward views of nihilism, atheism, and death. God makes no sense because when reality is meaningless; either everything is true or nothing is true. Relativists will therefore ask, "How can these several religions all be true, if everything is true?" or will find that truth changes. And so we are led, again, to the fact that if truth changes, then everything is up to me and my own internal arbitration; I must worship myself and my rationality rather than a doubtful God.

Ward therefore claims that the internet, with its presumed boundlessness of both space and desire, cannot be an art form because it does not participate in the transcendent – in good, truth, and beauty, which are traditional avenues by which philosophers and theologians have contemplated God. Note that Ward does not think that the internet really is boundless, and this, too, is important in understanding the idolatry of the internet. Because it is developed and controlled by the wealthy, and especially by free-market capitalism, the internet only appears limitless but is actually bounded by rules and regulations of the few. The view of boundlessness serves the gods of capitalism and consumerism,

---

[22] Graham Ward, *Cities of God* (London: Routledge Press, 2000), 253.

[23] For example, postmodern feminists have sometimes asked if there is such a thing as "gender" or whether that is a marker of identity entirely constructed by the cultures of which we are part.

among others, and it reinforces "worship" of those gods exactly by
enabling its users to think they are entering freeing space.

Ward does not thereby think we must succumb to the idea that
the internet will simply swallow our world whole and spit out a
virtual sub-par commercialized world. He thinks instead that
theology could have the resources to tell the story about the internet
and us differently. Ward argues that one way theology can describe
the internet is by analogy. On his view, the theologian should
narrate the internet in terms that make it analogical to practices
of the church, especially practices of embodiment.[24] That is to say,
analogically, the internet shows us what we humans lack, both in
cyberspace and in the "real world" – and it shows us we will always
lack until the *eschaton*: Truth, Beauty, Good, and Justice.

Ward hits important points, especially in his uncovering of the
ways the internet deceives people into thinking they are free, as
well as in his intuition that theology done as analogy can help us
understand ourselves more truthfully. He suggests that we think
about our world in relation to Augustine's two cities, the City of
God and the earthly city. These cities are intermixed so that

> [n]one of us can know the extent to which any activity we are
> engaged in is a work in God, and therefore good and true and
> beautiful, or a work of self-reference, and therefore nothing but
> the swollen bruising of an injury to the body.[25]

For him, there is always ambiguity in how the City of God makes
itself known in this life, which is why he deems the concept of
analogy so necessary. Theologians (among others) should always be
on the lookout for the connections, comparisons, and dissimilarities
with truth, beauty, and goodness, all the while seeking where new
forms of power and oppression have been put into place by new
technologies or other entities that displace the City of God.

Given Ward's arguments, it is curious that the internet is almost
solely described in negative terms, set in analogous contrast to the local,
embodied practices of churches. He chides theologians for having a
falsely placed nostalgia that "sacralizes concepts, objects, forms and
states from the past and then reproduces them in a present that simulates

---

[24] Ward, *Cities of God*, 256.

[25] Ibid.

and commodifies their pastness."[26] Yet, is his own focus on embodied local cultures also nostalgic, to an extent, and also open to the charge of idolatry? In other words, could analogical theology of the kind Ward describes fully read and engage online arguments like Bauer's, where she is directly suggesting a different view of objects, forms, and concepts and where she is perhaps taming the power of the internet?

The internet indeed mirrors our post-Enlightenment, consumer, global society in many of the ways that Ward suggests. But does it mirror those assumptions because it, itself, *is* a mirror, merely capable of reflecting what happens in "real life," but because it is only a mirror, being detached from truth and beauty? Or does it mirror those assumptions because its forms can be analogically compared to offline life in such a way that we can make observations about offline life that we could not have made prior to the advent of the internet? Ward privileges the former view of the internet ("one participates in the illusions of freedom and infinity"[27]), yet Bauer's blog posts make a strong case for the latter view, both in form and in content.

This is not to say that there is no idolatry on the web; quite the contrary. Hipps and Pickell both make good cases to that effect, and I would not want to eschew the embodiment that the church offers. But it is to extend Ward's own argument to suggest that, indeed, theologians need to be describing analogies, but those analogies are not about comparing internet life in a negative way to the embodied localities of Christians. The internet is not likely to be a proper site for participating in the sacraments or other physical forms of materiality that signify God's grace, but that does not mean that the internet is incapable of offering some fruitful theological discourse and signs of beauty. The two cities are mixed, both in online and offline discourse. Internet conversations are constrained in certain ways but differently than in offline theological discourse.

Beauty and truth

The arguments about idolatry and the internet recall another time and place when Christians were concerned with images,

---

[26] Ward, "Between Virtue and Virtuality," 55.

[27] Ward, "Between Virtue and Virtuality", 65.

embodiment, beauty, and truth. The iconoclasm movement of the eight century arose out of concern about the veneration of icons in worship. The concern centered on the Old Testament prohibition of idolatrous images, in contrast to the view that, by becoming man, God had entered into history for all time and therefore scandalously becomes matter worthy of worship. John of Damascus, one of the key theologians writing in favor of icons, suggests that a change occurs in the way humans can respond and relate to God: before the incarnation, God had no body, but after the incarnation, God can be represented by matter and form. The questions raised were not about matter as such, but about whether matter could be used in relation to worship of God. "I do not adore the creation rather than the Creator, but I adore the one who became a creature, who was formed as I was, who clothed Himself in creation without weakening or departing from His divinity. . . ."[28] Could mere creation truly honor the creator of all? John of Damascus argues that it can.

Part of his argument stems from considering all the ways in which bodies interact with their environments. The importance of matter and the body in worship of God is:

> [W]e are fashioned of both soul and body, and our souls are not naked spirits, but are covered, as it were, with a fleshly veil, it is impossible for us to think without using physical images. Just as we physically listen to perceptible words in order to understand spiritual things, so also by using bodily sight we reach spiritual contemplation. For this reason Christ assumed both soul and body, since man [sic] is fashioned from both. Likewise baptism is both of water and of Spirit. It is the same with communion, prayer, psalmody, candles, or incense; they all have a double significance, physical and spiritual.[29]

Idolatry in John Damascene's time was linked to the precise physical nature of things; the wood and paint on which a person could behold images of God led to idolatry. The brilliant point that John

---

[28] John of Damascus, *On the Divine Images: Three Apologies Against Those Who Attack the Divine Images* (Crestwood, NY: St Vladimir's Seminary Press, 1997), 15.

[29] John of Damascus, 72–3.

of Damascus makes in the above passage though, is that humans encounter everything via their bodies: even those things that people suppose are not idolatrous, such as the words of scripture read aloud.

By contrast, what is so interesting about the arguments of idolatry on and off the internet is that the fact of human bodies seems to have dropped out of the argument and we are discussing, instead, media as though they function apart from human bodies. Note that Bauer, for example, is concerned about writing over against what she sees as an image-based digital world. Hipps is concerned with embodiment in almost exactly the ways the iconoclasts were: there are certain ways in which matter is not idolatrous, and that way includes very particular forms of embodiment: reading scripture, being the church in sacraments and good acts. Ward, too, speaks of the embodiment of local church practices as holy in contradistinction to the realities of the internet.

The difficulty with all of the arguments presented so far is that they describe human life as dichotomous in relation to the internet – as though they are entirely separate. This is not ever how humans encounter the world, however, including the virtual spaces in which they participate. The internet simply does not happen without human bodies in some way employing themselves, senses included, at the keyboard or phone or manipulating the robots that sometimes operate in internet spaces too. Indeed, internet spaces are beginning to incorporate programs where body language like kissing can be communicated in some way, along with videos and written text.[30] It is not the fact that the internet exists that is the question here, though that is how the conversation is defined. Rather it is that we have a hard time conceiving the internet as matter and as part of our world because it both is, and is not, like the images in paintings and the writings in books.

Naming the internet as aesthetic allows it to sometimes be analogous with other facets of human life (and Christian

---

[30] The Kajimoto lab in Japan has developed a technology that allows people to kiss – albeit not in the usual way. This is not embodied in the usual offline way, but it does involve a body and ought to make us think further about what it means to be embodied creatures. See "Japan Lab Develops Remote Kissing Device," *GMA News Online*, (May 3, 2011) http://www.gmanews.tv/story/219493/technology/japan-lab-develops-remote-kissing-device. Accessed July 7, 2011.

discipleship) and sometimes not, incorporating the salient points of Ward's argument. It also allows for judgment about whether its purposes, at a given time, are good or bad. Because what is aesthetic deals with a range of participation in the Beautiful, there are points at which we can see the internet as more tool than art. At the same time, we can see that there are times in which the internet is more art than tool.

For example, people make judgments about the aesthetic appeal of the design of web pages and the use of pictures and animated characters in blogs and signatures. The Google search engine is one example: its portal is deceptively simple and yet inviting. The page is not cluttered with extraneous material, but only displays a simple text box. The beauty of this website is that the search engine performs well: one can type in entire strings of words without worrying about using the clunky Boolean operators "and," "not," and quotation marks. Computers, and the internet with them, contain many different aesthetic styles and questions. Even in the foundational stories of computing, the aesthetic nature comes across, in the differences between IBM and Macintosh, where Macintosh was often described as more user-friendly and intuitive. IBM computers, however, were simple, no-nonsense computers that eschewed frills. Today, these aesthetic styles are still present in the differences between PC and Mac, between Linux and Microsoft. Internet interfaces, too, have become part of aesthetic judgment. One tongue-in-cheek website says: "Microsoft leaves no doubt what their products are. If they made toilet paper, it would be called Butt Wiper. . . [Firefox] is a much cooler name."[31] BBspot compares the graphics as well. Internet Explorer's graphic symbol of an E is deemed boring and "utilitarian"; Firefox's graphic is "cool."

In the everyday language people use to describe the internet, there is an underlying sense of aesthetic judgment and therefore a sense of what is "appropriate" activity for the internet. I suspect that Ward would be concerned with this depiction in part because the aesthetic judgments about Firefox and Internet Explorer relate to consumer desire – what is "cool." As many theologians have suggested, however, when Christians conform to consumer desires and consumer culture,

---

[31] Brian Briggs, "Browser Showdown: Firefox vs. Internet Explorer," at *BBspot*, (January 20, 2005) http://www.bbspot.com/News/2005/01/firefox_vs_internet_explorer.html. Accessed June 1, 2006.

they are prone to putting those desires (even unknowingly) ahead of desire for God. Note, though, that while consumer desire is indeed a part of the judgment about these browsers, there is more: one of the critiques about Internet Explorer is that it is utilitarian and efficient. Firefox, by contrast, is open source technology, free to any and all who seek it. Firefox thus resists, to an extent, consumer culture, by being a gift shared by tech-savvy people interested in seeing what new things they can design and create.

So, the internet is part of aesthetic judgments and aesthetic culture in ways similar to how artists are part of aesthetic cultures. I use the word "aesthetic" in a premodern sense: the aesthetic, that which is beauty, is transcendental, and is a referent to God who is the Beautiful. We humans and other creatures can participate in the Beautiful and we have a share in it. All that is harmony and order among humans shares in what is wholly beautiful, and moreover, what is beautiful unites all who participate in it. Beauty, in the premodern sense, draws everything to itself out of love, and for this reason, what is Beautiful is related to what is Good. The internet, as a human creation much like a painting is a human creation, is a medium that can allow us humans to participate in this Beauty because the internet itself is deemed capable of having qualities of beauty itself. Beauty is a form of knowledge or a way of understanding the world, and it is therefore related to truth, which also links with knowledge;[32] as we saw in some of the Web 2.0 theological conversations, assessment of truth is one way of assessing beauty, and vice versa.[33]

So the internet can be a way toward contemplation of God. Jacques Maritain suggests that Christian art is "the art of humanity redeemed":[34] it does not necessarily depict "ecclesiastical" scenes or ideas but instead,

> [e]verything, sacred and profane, belongs to it. It is at home in the whole range of [human] industry and joy. Symphony or ballet, film or novel, landscape or still life, vaudeville or opera,

[32] Jacques Maritain, *Art and Scholasticism, With Other Essays*, trans J. F. Scanlan (New York: Charles Scribner's Sons, 1930), 3.

[33] All of the transcendentals are linked with each other and I am sure that each could provide interesting fodder for this chapter. My focus on beauty and truth arises specifically from the question of idolatry and so that provides my focus.

[34] Jacques Maritain, *Art and Scholasticism*, 68.

it can be as apparent in them all as in the stained-glass windows and statues of churches.[35]

So, too, with the internet.

The aesthetic nature of an art work not only can provide an avenue toward contemplating God, but it also links us with the created world and forms and conforms us to certain views of that world. In this way, what is aesthetic participates in theological life. For example, a chapel on the campus of the liberal arts school where I used to teach is a building that was designed by a Presbyterian architect to be both chapel and campus auditorium. In keeping with Calvinist theology, the walls are bare. Outwardly, the building looks like a small replica of a Jewish temple as the architect imagined it, with lots of pillars, in keeping with the Biblical emphasis on the temple as the place where God resides. The space dictates the activity of the participants, and thus forms them in a sense. Many forms of music, art, and ritual activity are eschewed by this space, for example. There is no room for paraments to drape the lectern, and no room for a choir, band, or organ. The congregation finds small ways to resist the space, by bringing in musicians who must stand awkwardly in the aisles while they play, or by taping paraments with the liturgical colors to the stone lectern. Still, the congregation knows that it is stymied in its attempts to bring art and music into the space unless they tear down the building and build again. Their resistance is only a token effort in a space that means to have them pray in silence and sing acapella. The building itself compels people to think about and worship God in very particular ways.

Just as with the artistic form of the liberal arts college chapel, the internet mediates space and compels us to think in particular ways. Architecture seems an apt metaphor to use in thinking about internet "space"; just as architects manipulate space to create certain moods and effects, so the internet spaces mediate how we think about and respond to our world. It therefore also mediates our access to truth and other transcendentals in ways that are clearly not confined to the internet alone. Sherry Turkle describes this phenomenon in her book *Life on the Screen*:

---

[35] Maritain, 69.

Why is it so hard for me to turn away from the screen?...When I write at the computer. . .my thinking space seems some how enlarged. The dynamic layered display gives me the comforting sense that I write in conversation with my computer. . . . There is something else that keeps me at the screen. I feel pressure from a machine that seems itself to be perfect and leaves no one and no other thing but me to blame.[36]

For Turkle, the computer represents a longing for perfection and order, both aspects of what counts as "aesthetic".

So why do people believe that the internet is boundless and limitless? Precisely because their experience of the space is that there is always a possibility for starting a new page, a new blog, a new discussion; there are always new links to new spaces they have not been. There are more things to experience on the internet than we can possibly manage to learn in a lifetime. But consider: the same could be said of offline life in the sense that there are far more books published, people to meet, places to visit than we can ever hope to do or see in a lifetime. Our experiences of offline life, however, are mediated by the way our bodies experience the spaces: in books that have a beginning and end, in buildings that are finite. By contrast, this space looks infinite, but it only *looks* so.

We are still learning what kinds of limits and boundaries internet life does have. The recent revelation that a Syrian female blogger questioning her sexuality turned out to be a man from the United States, is a case in point.[37] The incident stands as a reminder that the aesthetic of the internet conceals some kinds of knowledge about the world, though it was exactly because of inconsistencies and fake photos that the hoax came to light. Tom MacMaster, the creator of the blog, claimed to want only the best and also claimed that he had not (really) instigated any harm toward anyone. He seems to have succumbed to naïveté about the internet. He thought of it as

---

[36] Sherry Turkle, *Life on the Screen: Identity in the Age of the Internet* (New York: Simon and Schuster, 1997), 29.

[37] See "Gay Syrian Female Blogger Hoax," YouTube (June 13, 2011) http://www.youtube.com/watch?v=o_TTKfAZBfw and "A Gay Girl in Damascus," *AlJazeera* online, (June 13, 2011) http://english.aljazeera.net/news/middleeast/2011/06/20116 71229558865.html for brief accounts of how far the hoax went. Both sites accessed June 15, 2011.

merely a space in which he could manipulate his identity, because of the internet's boundless and open aesthetic. But this "mere" space affects real people and places, including nation-state politics.

The aesthetic of boundless, limitless space has particular analogies in theology. Scholastic theology itself had a form, the disputation, made most famous by Thomas Aquinas' *Summa Theologica* and which was seen as appropriate for theological discourse about faith and reason. The disputation form began with a theological question. The scholar would first show how other scholars had attempted to answer that question. Then the author would provide his own answer to the question, followed by rebuttals, critiques or addendums to the other authors' answers, written in such a way that everything supported his own answer to the question. The first question raised would spawn other questions and so the theological enterprise as conceived by Scholastics ended up being an infinite delving into the mysteries of God. The form circumscribes the way theology is done; subsequent theologians would find the disputation to be constraining for their purposes such that contemporary theology rarely takes the form of a disputation, though scholars still examine others' arguments and begin papers by asking questions.

The aesthetic of the disputational form provides an analogy for interpreting theological discussion on the internet in because of the way the internet does not have an end to it. Unlike doing theology in the medium of a book, which has a first page and a last page, there is not that kind of beginning or ending on the internet, which relates to the infinite nature of theology. David Bentley Hart writes,

> True beauty is not the idea of the beautiful, a static archetype in the 'mind of God, but is an infinite 'music,' drama, art, completed in – but never 'bounded' by – the termless dynamism of the Trinity's life; God is boundless, and so is never a boundary; his music possesses the richness of every transition, interval, measure, variation – all dancing and delight.[38]

On the internet, there are portals: home pages and search engines in which people can constantly and continuously ask questions, making theological enterprise seem infinite. Like the disputational form,

---

[38] David Bentley Hart, *The Beauty of the Infinite: The Aesthetics of Christian Truth* (Grand Rapids, MI: Eerdmans, 2003), 177.

the internet's supposed boundlessness invites quests for knowledge. However, such knowledge often becomes truncated. One of the key differences between the internet and the disputational form is that internet theologians are not as likely to seek out (or to know how to seek out) the range of good opinions on the question. As I will discuss in Chapter 4, it is not clear that people are able to stake out the best of the range of opinions and intelligibly use them in their arguments, in the same way that it is impossible for me to give a summation of theological conversation done on the web. I can only provide snapshots for my particular account and argument. (One could ask similarly, though, whether scholastics were quite able to provide a range of scholarly opinion and adjudicate the tradition. The best of them might do so, but not everyone was Thomas Aquinas.)

Still, to write off the internet as simply incapable of conveying anything about beauty or truth or God is to be strangely unaware of our own place as creatures with bodies that are engaged with the world even at the same time as the world shapes and forms us. The internet is part of creation by virtue of the fact that we are part of creation. Ward uses Augustine's two cities to describe human life in postmodern context; internet itself bears the marks of the two cities. Not everything is part of God's city, and understanding the internet (at least partly) as an aesthetic form is to be able to evaluate it. As Bauer notes:

> There are aspects of digital culture that we should fight against, not because they are 'not print' but because they are not godly:
>
> The anonymity which allows us to lie and deceive each other;
>
> The easy access to pornography which allows us to take part in the degredation [sic], the use, the exploitation, of those with less power, and which poisons our own relationships;
>
> The overwhelming encouragement to spend and spend and spend. (Nobody ever talks about the demonic aspects of that "one click" button.)[39]

By contrast, Bauer makes a largely successful argument about internet theological inquiry being able to critique offline idolatry of words. Similarly, people do find the internet to be a fruitful place for thinking about questions. Saying that the internet is part of embodied

---

[39] Susan Wise Bauer, ibid.

life is not to sidestep questions about the critiques Ward makes, but it is to say that despite all that there can be the possibility of something beneficial – at least in this earthly city – coming from this material.

God and God's Creature, the Internet

summatheologiae Thomas Aquinas[40]

"1.6.2 ad 3. God is outside genus, the principle of every genus; God is compared to others by excess, which is what the supreme good implies."

Having said all of this, I have still mostly spoken about human life and have spoken very little about God. There is good reason for this, which I can perhaps sum up with one of "Thomas Aquinas'" 140-character tweets. While I'm not sure that all of the tweets do justice to his great work, the *Summa Theologica*, I think the one quoted above maintains a key point. "God is outside genus." I would go on to add: God is the *only one* outside genus; everything else, the internet included, is part of the created world. In the case of the internet, it is part of the created world by virtue of being part of human life. This fact, too, reminds us that we cannot simply shunt the internet into a corner and proclaim it as disembodying and disembodied in the ways that some have wanted to see it. Nor can we do the opposite, and proclaim that the internet is doing something entirely new and fascinating. To do either of these is to start toward a slippery slope, for that view suggests that the web, like God, is outside genus.

It is very difficult to think about something as outside genus. This is, I think, part of the difficulty in New Atheism discussions. Hemant Mehta, a self-proclaimed atheist, suggests that atheists therefore frame questions in what can be known, rather than resorting to what he sees as wild stories. He writes,

> It's not that atheists know everything; it's just that we're perfectly comfortable saying 'We don't know' to questions that no one has

---

[40] *Thomas Aquinas @ Summa Theologiae: Tweeting One Article a Day for Your Amusement and Edification*, (September 11, 2010) http://twitter.com/#%21/ summatheologiae. Accessed June 15, 2011.

the answer to. Why do we exist at all? I don't know. What caused the Big Bang? I don't know. Why do we have consciousness? I don't know. I don't know those things and you don't either.[41]

These are genuinely human questions and indeed, good questions to ask.

However, a great many answers to these questions rely on a belief that God must necessarily manifest to the world in ways that are observable to the world. So, the so-called "new atheists" tend to draw arguments along the lines of physical supporting evidence, which is merely the material of which this world is made. The question for Mehta and others, therefore, is why it is acceptable to ask questions about proofs of God, but unacceptable to ask a question like, "Why does the world exist?" He seems to be closing off particular kinds of inquiry arbitrarily, especially since evidentiary proofs are, themselves, mediated by human experience and understanding such that like all human knowledge, they are fallible. Theologian Herbert McCabe suggests, "a genuine atheist is one who simply does not see that there is any problem or mystery here, one who is content to ask questions within the world, but cannot see that the world itself raises a question."[42]

McCabe suggests that God is "an answer to our ultimate question, how come anything instead of nothing?"[43] Yet McCabe goes on to reason that if God is an answer to "how come anything?" God must not therefore be thought of as an object in our universe. We cannot think of God as a "thing" and so we quickly discover that most of our language is theologically inadequate because it is very difficult, if not impossible, to use language and not refer to *things*. What is even more difficult is to remember that our human conceptions of God are inadequate. For instance, God does not have a "life" – God is life.

By contrast, technology is often seen in terms of genus, species, and so on. We make distinctions on the basis of apparent progress and newness: film, car, plane, radio, television, computer, internet,

[41] Hemant Mehta, "Ask an Atheist... (Hemant Reponds)" *Rachel Held Evans: Author, Speaker, Blogger*, (July 5, 2011) http://rachelheldevans.com/ask-an-atheist-response. Accessed July 5, 2011.

[42] Herbert McCabe, *God Matters* (London: Mowbray, 1987), 7.

[43] Ibid., 6.

iphone, and so on. The differences between these things seem huge, especially as each new technology comes along and each successive generation tends to make a big deal about these differences (and often rightly so). But when it comes to contrasts between these things and God, all of these technologies are still merely part of the world, still merely creatures. Whatever humans have created, they have done as humans. This has added much to human life, on human terms. But it has added nothing to God, nor has it detracted anything from God.

However, when we think with wonder of the fact that God chooses to conform to human life, as Jesus, God's becoming a creature in a world of creatures means that there is a change in the world. That change is that the world is redeemed through matter. All of material life becomes bound up in the possibilities that Jesus brings, even future forms that no first-century Palestinian Jew could have conceived. So, the internet, as part of this material world, as part of human life, has possibilities of redemption too. That is a good thing, for as Bauer mentions, there are plenty of things on the internet that pinpoint the need for redemption. And, as a creature along with us, as a mirror of our offline lives, the medium of the internet may teach us to see better those things that are not healthy parts of life.

In this chapter I have focused on the internet as multiple artworks done in multiple media, emphasizing the materiality of the internet and, as such, its relationship to God. Yet such a view of the internet is inadequate, even if true. The internet is not only an art form, it is a form of life. In part III of Bauer's blog post, commenter Jason argues with Bauer's particular assumptions about the written word and the image, claiming: "The essential shift is not in the movement from text to graphics or from length to brevity, but rather from isolation to accessibility." Human beings turn to the internet for connections and community and not just for information or aesthetics. So, what becomes of humanity when it is seen in light of the internet? It is to that question we now turn.

3

Theological cyborgology in Aquinas on the Web?

Frugal Trenches, a blog post "On Lent and Things":

And while I don't think Lent should be about setting yourself unrealistic goals, I do believe it should be a time of sacrifice, change, renewal, mourning and re-birth. So I've set up a little plan, for Lent I will:

- Take a full 24 hour media fast (no internet at home and no tv) each week
- No sugar (aka no candy, chocolate, biscuits, scones yada yada)
- At least two, 2 hr walks each week
- Swimming each day
- At least 1 hr prayer or Bible reading a day – using my prayer calendar.[1]

---

[1] Frugal Trenches, "On Lent and Things," at *Notes from the Frugal Trenches – A Downshifting Journey,* (March 8, 2011) http://notesfromthefrugaltrenches. com/2011/03/08/on-lent-and-things. Accessed May 17, 2011.

Comment by MsDerious:

Most of us reading this post are incredibly lucky, the very fact we have access to the internet suggests we also have access to things like clean water, medical help and a safe place to sleep at nights. That makes us more fortunate than a massive amount of the world.[2]

The internet conversation: Internet fasts and *Avatar*

Unlike other theological conversations (like those about authority or church) discussed online, which often look like their offline counterparts, theological anthropology does not present itself in typical ways. I imagine that is partly because theological anthropology asks us to investigate ourselves in light of how God has revealed God's self to us. How are we to investigate what the internet means for us and does to us as humans in relation to God, though, when we are in the middle of it?

Even theologian bloggers do not reflect on what it means to be human, made by God, on the web. Interesting theological anthropology conversations happen in less obvious ways, such as the conversation presented above at Frugal Trenches' blog. "Turning off" for prescribed periods of time thus becomes a way out, a way to reflect on the meaning of technology for one's self while remaining in its midst. Another area where reflection about what it means to be human happens is in Christians' conversations about the godliness of movies, such as the Harry Potter series or *Avatar*.

In this chapter, I examine a sampling of theological conversations about Lenten fasting, as well as the movie *Avatar*, to show what questions online theological conversations raise about what it means to be human. Based on these questions, I examine the question of whether we internet/social media-using humans might now be better named "cyborgs" – half human and half machine. Finally, I discuss what implications that has for offline theological anthropologies.

---

[2] MsDerious, Comment, "On Lent and Things," at *Notes from the Frugal Trenches*, (March 9, 2011) http://notesfromthefrugaltrenches.com/2011/03/08/on-lent-and-things. Accessed May 17, 2011.

While Christians have responded to the internet in largely positive ways, every year during Lent a significant number also turn themselves off from the web or from specific parts of the web, like Facebook. Why is this the case?

Frugal Trenches sees a 24-hour media fast as related to her Lenten goals of "sacrifice, change, renewal, mourning, and re-birth." The point about sacrifice might seem obvious: disconnecting from the web seems daunting to many, to the point of being very much a sacrifice. But the metaphors of rebirth, change, and renewal suggest something else: disconnecting from the web and other media enables re-formation as a human being. Somehow, media have encroached on some basic point of being human, though Frugal Trenches does not delineate what that might be.

Frugal Trenches' language in her blog post suggests a disquiet with her "self" as she speaks about wanting a "re-birth." Rebirth is a good term to use for a Lenten fast. Lent's journey leads us toward the cross and resurrection; it is meant to remind us of our baptism, when we ourselves were baptized into Jesus' life, death, and resurrection.[3] And baptism is meant to make us new creatures, having been reborn into a new way of life. So it is interesting, then, that Frugal Trenches sees a need for rebirth in relation to her internet use. In fact, in a later blog post, Frugal Trenches decides that a 24-hour fast is not enough:

> I know how I want to live and it isn't with people I love remembering me on the internet or watching tv. I read an article recently which said the average mother is on facebook, twitter, blogs, forums or yahoo groups for more than 3 hours each day during their child's waking hours (many more during their non-waking hours), often in short bursts so they don't realize how distracted they are.[4]

These are incisive words, especially coming from someone who regularly blogs (and who continued to blog before and after both of these posts).

---

[3] Romans 6, for example.

[4] Frugal Trenches, "Reclaiming Simple Sundays," at *Notes from the Frugal Trenches – A Downshifting Journey*, (March 13, 2011) http://notesfromthefrugaltrenches. com/2011/03/13/reclaiming-simple-sundays-20/. Accessed May 17, 2011.

What is even more interesting is MsDerious' comment on Frugal Trenches' original post. She makes a move to remind Frugal Trenches and her blog readers of other people who do not have the "luck" of connecting online. MsDerious thereby raises a question about what it means to be a person online in relation to other people who are not able to be online. From MsDerious' point of view, online people have a kind of power and ability that others do not have. Online people have choices, and from MsDerious' point of view, making a choice to turn away from the internet is a positive one that helps people reconnect with non-internet-using people.

"Turning off" for Lent can lead to some pretty intense soul-searching. Elizabeth Foss, writing online for the *Arlington Catholic Herald*: "What if. What if instead of reading 300 words here and there all over the internet all day long, I just read one book at a time? One hundred fifty pages or more of complete thoughts and careful writing. Would I stop thinking in those short, snippy, often snarky phrases that mirrored what I'd read online?"[5] Foss acknowledges that her online encounters might possibly be affecting the rest of her life. "Would I have more time. . .Would I connect with others. . .?" she wonders, as she contemplates turning away from the internet for prescribed periods of time each day.

Sara Annette responds to Foss in the way so many people do when confronted with turning away from the internet, or at least some form of social media:

> Great article! For me, the Internet has become my primary means of contact communications, so for me to fast from it the entire [L]enten season would be difficult and worry some folks. But I am considering, after reading your thoughts, about fasting one day a week as I do for Fridays from meat. Thanks![6]

Sara Annette neatly pinpoints the objection to such a fast: the internet is a form of communication. People, real people, might worry

---

[5] Elizabeth Foss, "An Internet Fast for Lent?" *Arlington Catholic Herald*, (February 24, 2010) http://www.catholicherald.com/opinions/detail.html?sub_id=12424. Accessed May 17, 2011.

[6] SaraAnnette, Comment, "An Internet Fast for Lent?" *Arlington Catholic Herald*, (February 24, 2010) http://www.catholicherald.com/opinions/detail.html?sub_id=12424. Accessed May 17, 2011.

if she dropped out of contact with them. Sara Annette's comment highlights how inextricably intertwined her life is with the internet such that turning away from it, even briefly, would be equivalent to disappearing for 40 days. It is interesting that Sara Annette does not consider using her communication devices to *communicate* a possible fast from the internet. Rather, it is impossible for her to imagine going without because that is simply who she is.

Jenni makes a different point about human life in relation to cutting down on internet activity:

> This week I've made a conscious choice to cut down on the amount of internet in my life. . . . I've found browsing the internet has become my default activity when I come in from work – and that's NOT what I want it to be! Yes, I have joined communities and made beautiful friends through the internet, several of whom I've met up with in person, and all of whom are very supportive, but the amount of time I spend is preventing me from doing the things I went looking for inspiration for in the first place (baking bread, making food, gardening, sewing, living simply. . .).[7]

Jenni acknowledges that internet communities have led to a certain kind of connectivity with other people, but those online relationships have also taken her away from some offline activities. Interestingly, in naming these offline activities, Jenni names precisely those kinds of activities that Albert Borgmann as focal practices in Chapter 1: concrete practices that enable a person to withstand technological encroachment on their life.

Of course, there are numerous Christians who find an internet fast to be a mere token practice in a decidedly technological age. Elizabeth Drescher, author of *Tweet if You Heart Jesus*, writes sardonically on her blog: "Ah, the social media fast—the latest expression of our collective wrestling with the digital angel."[8]

---

[7] Jenni, Comment on "Reclaiming Simple Sundays," at *Notes from the Frugal Trenches – A Downshifting Journey,* (March 13, 2011) http://notesfromthefrugaltrenches. com/2011/03/13/reclaiming-simple-sundays-20. Accessed May 17, 2011.

[8] Elizabeth Drescher, "Digital Dust-up: Lenten Practice in the Digital Reformation," at *Elizabeth Drescher, PhD,* (March 19, 2011) http://www.elizabethdrescher.net/ ElizabethdrescherNet/My_Blog/Entries/2011/3/19_Digital_Dust-Up__Lenten_ Practice_in_the_Digital_Reformation.html. Accessed May 16, 2011.

The trouble, for Drescher, is that these internet fasts, among other things, seem too embedded in "hipster" Christian culture, where it is posh to give up the internet and show a kind of consumer-type faithfulness only because others are doing it too. "In this light," she says, "it doesn't much matter if you give up Facebook during Lent—though there surely may be many spiritual benefits if you undertake your digital fast reflectively. To the extent you still live and work and love and worship in the world, you remain plugged into to a culture in the midst of a remarkable transformation with tremendous spiritual and ecclesial implications."[9] Drescher implies that we cannot really remove ourselves from the internet – much as some of the technological theologians and philosophers I mention in Chapter 1 have discussed the impossibility of seeing ourselves as separate from a technological worldview.

Along similar lines as what MsDerious notes above, Drescher discusses how the social media fast might well take someone away from their online community.[10] More strangely, Drescher suggests that a social media fast might prevent people from facing fears they have about the internet by "vacationing" from a technology that they have not yet made part of their lives. This is odd, for it is not the people who currently do not use social media who proclaim fasts from them; it is people who are concerned that something about social media is taking them away from themselves, as those bloggers mentioned above suggest. The internet somehow makes us seem less human to ourselves.

Compare these conversations about Lenten fasts with some of the conversations about the movie *Avatar*. *Avatar* is intriguing to consider in relation to web technology, in any case, because the movie's title makes use of a widespread web-based term used to refer

---

[9] Ibid.

[10] I note here that there are very real questions about whether Christians on the internet are really part of communities, which I discuss in more detail in Chapter 6 where I write about ecclesiology. But there is also the question of whether Christians are obliged to be part of communities. A passage from Dietrich Bonhoeffer's book *Life Together* comes to mind: "It is not simply to be taken for granted that the Christian has the privilege of living among other Christians. Jesus Christ lived in the midst of his enemies. At the end all his disciples deserted him. On the Cross he was utterly alone, surrounded by evildoers and mockers. . . . So the Christian, too, belongs not in the seclusion of a cloistered life but in the thick of foes." (New York: Harper & Row Publishers, 1954), 7.

to a person's online persona (and, of course, the web-based term is itself derived from religious Sanskrit terminology, an interesting use of metaphor in its own right that I do not have space to discuss here). A web-based avatar can be as simple as an email address or an IM handle, but it most often refers to visual virtual representations of beings (not necessarily human beings) such as those found in Second Life and World of Warcraft. *Avatar* is also fascinating for Christians because of its clear references to Christian people and principles. For example, one blogger writes: "Consider the name of the scientist played by Sigourney Weaver: 'Grace Augustine.' Is Cameron giving us a little hint that the film may have something more up its religious sleeve than the Gospel of Sustainability?"[11]

Much internet debate about the film derives from an op-ed piece written by *New York Times* columnist Ross Douthat, called "Heaven and Nature." Douthat argues that *Avatar* is Hollywood's latest defense of pantheism, a religion that "calls humanity into religious communion with the natural world."[12] In the film, Ewya is described as the life energy that all nature shares; human-like creatures like the Na'vi renew themselves by plugging their USB port-like hair into an Ewya tree. Americans like the idea of pantheism, says Douthat, precisely because of their relationship with technology: "We pine for what we've left behind, and divinizing the natural world is an obvious way to express unease about our hyper-technological society."[13] Then Douthat goes on to offer a scathing critique of this Americanized psyche to say that pantheistic religion overidolizes nature. Nature is not the peace-loving energy depicted in the movie; it is violent. On Douthat's view, those cultures that most resemble the Na'vi life are also the ones whose people have short, bestial lives. So he continues, "Religion exists, in part, precisely because humans aren't at home amid these cruel rhythms. We stand half inside the natural world and half outside it."[14]

---

[11] Mark Silk, "Avatar's Christian theme" on "Spiritual Politics: A Blog on Religion and American Political Culture," (December 25, 2009) http://www.spiritual-politics. org/2009/12/avatars_christian_theme.html. Accessed April 18, 2011.

[12] Ross Douthat, "Heaven and Nature," *The New York Times Online*, (December 20, 2009) http://www.nytimes.com/2009/12/21/opinion/21douthat1.html. Accessed April 18, 2011.

[13] Ibid.

[14] Ibid.

Two aspects are interesting here: one is that Douthat associates Avatar's yearning for nature with an apologetic against technological society; the second is that Douthat links religion to humans who both belong to and exist apart from the natural world. Douthat's account of humanity seems, therefore, to be half natural, half technological/religious. Commenters on Douthat's essay tend either to agree wholeheartedly, that *Avatar* is an anti-Christian film, or to suggest that the Na'vi planet is merely another rendition of the Garden of Eden.[15]

Yet it is another New York Times op-ed blogger that pushes discussion forward even more. David Brooks suggests, "Every age produces its own sort of fables, and our age seems to have produced The White Messiah fable."[16] The fable goes something like: white man meets noble native people and emerges as their champion against the foes of his own culture. Brooks goes on to discuss in detail how *Avatar* produces its own White Messiah fable in the protagonist, James Cameron, who "becomes" a Na'vi by donning an avatar that he can put on and take off. J. Kameron Carter, a professional theologian at Duke University who also blogs, and writes in comment to Brooks: "This is an epic that has at its heart a basic question: Can white existence be save[d]? Can the white masculine be redeemed? Can it overcome its wounds, it wheel-chaired status?"[17] The question and possibility of human salvation is always on the edge of theological anthropology, though it is usually discussed as a doctrine in its own right, the doctrine of soteriology.

Commenter K. Grimes responds to Carter's question on this point: "What would the redemption of whiteness look like? since he rejects the avatar solution, what would it look like? basically, Carter's reading of avatar leads me to believe that he thinks it is impossible for white people to act in solidarity–that their whiteness

[15] See, for example, "Tim's" comment at http://northwardho.blogspot.com/2009/12/heaven-and-nature-ross-douhat-on-james.html. Accessed April 18, 2011.

[16] David Brooks, "The Messiah Complex," *The New York Times Online*, (January 7, 2010) http://www.nytimes.com/2010/01/08/opinion/08brooks.html?ref=opinion. Accessed June 3, 2011.

[17] J. Kameron Carter, "Avatar: An Amazing and Troubling Film" at *J. Kameron Carter*, (March 12, 2010) http://jkameroncarter.com/?p=56. Accessed June 3, 2011.

dooms them to damnation.(sic)"[18] A later commenter notes about K. Grimes' point:

> to K. Grimes question, what would 'the salvation of whiteness would look like?,' Avatar answers from within the resources of whiteness itself. . . . One is to realign himself with the brutal, imperial adventure that cost him his brother and crippled him (the leader promising him the funds to get new legs if he continues to cooperate). The other option is worked out through the Avatar, that is, through the imaginative and technological projection/ entrance into the space of the others, the Na'vi.[19]

One of the major questions that is raised by the film *Avatar* is the possibility of salvation in terms of technology, and thrown into the whole morass are questions of race and gender, such as those alluded to by Carter and his commenters.

These two web discussions show a tension about humanity and salvation: on the one hand, technology limits the human possibility to encounter God, to be fully human, and thus to be saved. On the other hand, technology is seen as "savior" but this in itself raises serious and troubling questions about race and gender, and thus about our abilities to interact with each other.

Theological anthropology?

"We've signed on to the notion that the best devices are those that deliver maximum connectedness. . .."[20]

It is easy to see where these internet conversations raise similar points as those raised by offline theologies. For example, what does

---

[18] K. Grimes, comment 1, (March 12, 2010) http://jkameroncarter.com/?p=56. Accessed June 3, 2011.

[19] Tim McGee, Comment, (March 14, 2010) http://jkameroncarter.com/?p=56. Accessed June 3, 2011.

[20] William Powers, *Hamlet's Blackberry: A Practical Philosophy for Building A Good Life in the Digital Age* (New York: Harper Collins, 2010), 123.

Thomas Aquinas know about human beings? Among other things, he knows that they are not God but have God as their source, he knows that they sin and are in need of salvation.[21] Humans are always in need of remembering their proper relationship to God. The contemporary field of theological anthropology has revolved around identity formation, raising much the same questions as James Cameron raises in *Avatar*. Black theology, Womanist and feminist theologies, postcolonial theology have all sought, in distinctive ways, to deal with the particularities of peoples' contexts for how they understand God's relationship with humans, as well as humans' relationships with each other.

Do we have essential identities as human beings? For example, God creates men and women in Genesis: How do we understand their creation in relation to gender roles? Are the biological parts the god-given parts, while roles are what humans have sinfully developed? Race and racism, too, have captivated theological attention. Is "race" a category created by human beings to subjugate other human beings? How can we understand race in relation to Christian identity and discipleship?[22] More recently, disability and sexuality have become part of the discussion of what it means to be human. Is being gay something inherent to one's being, a part of the person God made? Is disability a mark of being sinful, or angelic and innocent, or neither?

Theologians dealing particularly with scientific questions have also raised questions about what it means to be human. How much does DNA, or affinity with apes, or biochemical reactions count when it comes to identity? In thinking about identity, twentieth-century theologians have confronted evolution, genetics, and linguistic theory as well. Ian Barbour, for example, argues for seeing current movements in science as consistent with theological movements, particularly that of process theology.[23]

---

[21] See, for example, *Summa Theologica* I. II. qq. 74–84; 109–14.

[22] On this topic, see especially Willie James Jennings, *The Christian Imagination: Theology and the Origins of Race* (Hartford, CT: Yale University Press, 2011). See also J. Kameron Carter, *Race: A Theological Account* (New York: Oxford University Press, 2008).

[23] Ian G. Barbour, *Nature, Human Nature and God* (Minneapolis, MN: Fortress Press, 2002).

Into this broad array of conversations linked to theological anthropology, how does technology, and particularly the web, influence our continued discussion about human identity? In its own best view, it tries to overcome negative aspects of identity formation. A positive view of the internet supposes positive things about humans: "Online communities have often been celebrated as spaces that allow for an unbound human experience, spaces in which individuals are able to form identities and express themselves without the constraints found in the 'real world.'"[24] If the twentieth century was an age that discovered and dwelt on human distinctions, will the internet age be an age that tries to overcome them, or make them appear far less fixed than they have been?

This chapter argues, on the contrary, that all of the ways we humans have devised to keep each other as "other" remain in our internet discourse precisely because of the technology. Contemporary society not only replicates the negative aspects of cultural identity and so does little to mitigate theological anthropological questions about racism, sexism, able-ism, and the like. But it also denies even what Thomas Aquinas might have understood as a kind of theological anthropology, because our technology does not allow us to view ourselves as created by God, with God as our source, nor does it allow us to understand ourselves as sinners, particularly when it comes to perpetuating evils like racism.

The reason is because humans have become a different kind of creature on the web, a hybrid of human and technology. It may seem audacious to say it, but I think we have reached at least the beginnings of an Age of Cyborgs.[25] The opening quote for this section makes a claim about our understanding of technological devices: the best ones are the ones that instantaneously and constantly connect us to the web. As I participate on the internet, from my limited

---

[24] Robert Alan Brookey, "Paradise Crashed: Rethinking MMORPGs and Other Virtual Worlds, An Introduction," in *Critical Studies in Media Communications*, 26.2 (June 2009), 101.

[25] Thanks to my colleague Brad Kallenberg for initiating this conversation. See his book *God and Gadgets: Following Jesus in a Technological Age.* (Eugene, OR: Cascade Books, 2011). See also some of the early conversations about cyborgs and the ways in which humans and machines appear seamless: Donna Haraway, "A Cyborg Manifesto: Science, Technology, and Socialist-Feminism in the Late Twentieth Century," in her book *Simians, Cyborgs and Women: The Reinvention of Nature* (New York: Routledge, 1991), 149–81.

vantage point in web life, this rings true. Even more true is that we appear not to be able to disconnect ourselves from technology for very long. So thus, with a slight feeling of getting a bit too sci-fi, I argue that our conversation must now have to do with "theological cyborgology." What might this mean, in the context of theological anthropology? What might this mean for our relationship with God?

Humans and their (mere) tools?

In order to understand what I mean when I claim we have become cyborgs, we need to explore the ways we have tended to understand technology in relation to human beings. When I have discussed this book with people, more often than not they've shrugged and said something like, "Well, what's the big deal with the internet, anyway? Isn't it just kind of like the printing press and the Reformation?" One of the common stories is that the printing press is a tool, related to theological concerns in that it was largely responsible for the success of the Protestant Reformation. The printing press put far more books in the hands of lay people than ever before and a look at what kinds of books were being printed underscores the probability of a thesis about the printing press: Bibles and devotional literature topped the list of printed books. Scholarly books ranked too, but much farther behind.[26]

The commonplace thinking continues: Once lay people were able to have access to these kinds of books, there was no stopping a revolution. As they read their Bibles, they had questions about the way the dominant church structure operated. They wondered if that church could claim scriptural authenticity. Thus, when scripture scholars such as Jean Calvin wrote scriptural commentary, people could see that Calvin, with his scholarly background, was raising the kinds of questions that they, too raised. The Reformation thereby gained a momentum from popular support that it would not have

---

[26] Marshall McLuhan's book *The Gutenberg Galaxy.* (Toronto: University of Toronto Press, 1962) tells this story, though he is concerned with nonreligious ramifications too. Elizabeth Eisenstein's book *The Printing Press as an Agent of Change* (Cambridge: Cambridge University Press, 1980) more fully makes an argument about Christianity in relation to the printing press.

had, had books remained in the hands of scholars.[27] The printing press became a most excellent tool in developing theological thought.

By comparison, Elizabeth Drescher suggests that the internet is also a communication tool that puts information in the hands of the common people and that changes, positively, the ways we understand God and ourselves.

> Like the reformations of the twelfth and sixteenth centuries, the Digital Reformation has some revolutionary elements, but it is not about replacing one form of religious practice with another, in the way that eighteenth-century political revolutionaries in France and America sought to replace monarchy with democracy. . .Where the Digital Reformation is different. . .is that it is more plainly driven by the often ad hoc spiritualities of ordinary believers—clergy and laity alike—who have, on the one hand, new access to the resources of the Christian tradition not unlike those afforded by the printing press, but who, on the other, have access to technological means of connection, creativity, and collaboration with those resources that remained in the hands of a narrow élite even after the Protestant Reformations.[28]

Drescher makes a claim similar to the claims historians and philosophers of the printing press make about technology: developments in communication technology affect the ways we understand the world and hence affect our social interactions.

So, philosophers raise good questions about the affects of tools on human beings, and they wonder, rightly, what is the distinction between human and tool. For example, theologian Herbert McCabe writes about the telephone:

> Think of a telephone. There it is on the table, an object occupying a bit of your world, part of your visual space. You can do things to

---

[27] Of course, such a portrait is a bit misleading. It was not the case that prior to the printing press, lay people had no access to these books. There were scriptoria devoted to copying manuscripts intended for lay audiences.

[28] Elizabeth Drescher, *Tweet if You Heart Jesus* (New York: Morehouse, 2011), xviii.

it, move it or dust it. Now what happens when the telephone rings?
You pick it up and start talking and as you do this the telephone
ceases to be an object in front of you, a part of your world; it
becomes a means of communication with somebody, a means by
which you are with somebody. When it does that it disappears.[29]

As a tool, the telephone becomes part of our bodies when we use it
to communicate, but most of the time, we understand the telephone
as merely an object that we can put to use. We can use it at will.

The "printing press" view of the internet also affects the ways
people understand their bodies in relation to their tools. If the
printing press is a mere tool we take on and put off at will, some
have seen that we understand our bodies similarly, to be put on and
taken off at will. Wendell Berry has suggested that our technological
view understands the body as an encumbrance, and that technology
needs to be freed to ascend to heights our bodies could not achieve,
so much that we even favor technology over human contact.[30]
Travis Pickell, likewise, sees that the screen enables us to seemingly
disconnect from our bodies, which exacerbates a mind/body dualism.
Making use of a virtual medium such as the internet can only seem
to reinforce a mind/body dualism because avatars and emails seem
necessarily disembodied from our offline bodies that move and
breathe in spaces that are real, rather than metaphorical.

Others, like McCabe, suggest that the human body is the
antithesis of the tool. On McCabe's view, it is because "the body
is the source of communication that we say it is alive, that it has a
soul."[31] McCabe considers human beings as operating in the reverse
of the way the telephone works. McCabe would rather understand
the human body as a means of communication rather than an object
used for communication. The human body is not something we

---

[29] Herbert McCabe, *God Matters*. (London: Mowbray, 1987), 110.

[30] See, for example, Wendell Berry, "Why I am not going to buy a computer" in *What Are People For?* 2nd edition. (Berkeley, CA: Counterpoint Press, 2010), 170–7. Berry drew ire from people for this essay because he mentioned that his wife was the person who helped him with revising and editing his essays; people saw this as forcing servitude and continuing patriarchal norms. On Berry's view, however, it was not that his wife, as woman, was revising his essays, but that a human being, rather than a technological interface, was revising his essays.

[31] McCabe, 111.

can pick up and use at will, though some over the years have tried to make it so. If humans work in the ways that tools work, then humans, like tools, become objects. The telephone "disappears" and becomes a temporary part of the human body when it is used to communicate with others but the human body does not likewise merge with the telephone to become an object.

In either case – seeing humans as the opposite of tools, or seeing that tools help humans escape bodily encumbrances – there is an important dualism at work, different than the one Pickell suggests. This is the dualism (and the myth) of the human ability to be technologized or nontechnologized. Humans have depended on being able to make distinctions in tools/technology and themselves as human beings. Part of this is for psychological benefit. If humans began to understand themselves as tools, that moves them toward a view of humans as objects. Many theologians writing about the anthropological issues mentioned above, like gender, race, class, and disability, find themselves concerned exactly insofar as some humans end up seeming to be objects for other humans.

Conceiving of the internet as like the printing press/Protestant Reformation schema tends to limit people to thinking about the internet as a mere tool, like other technological tools – an important tool, one that drives social changes, but a tool nonetheless. After all, the printing press may have put books in the hands of more people, but the press itself remained a tool used by only a few. By contrast, the internet is used by many, and through its use, many are able to disseminate their ideas.[32] So what if we are wrong about our tools? Or what if the internet is more than a tool?

Becoming cyborgs

What if, instead, we find it hard to disengage and intelligibly separate our human bodies from our internet connections? How would we know that we are on the path to becoming part human,

---

[32] Importantly, though, the workings of computers and other devices that provide gateways to the internet remain mysterious. As Brad Kallenberg notes in *God and Gadgets*, only a generation or so ago, people could still take apart and put back together their tools themselves. With the rise of computers, and computerized phones, cars, et cetera, such a thing is now unthinkable. See especially Chapter 1 of his book.

part machine? In her book *Alone Together*, Sherry Turkle discusses the ways in which people find themselves treating robots as humans, while treating the humans they encounter online as objects.

Turkle describes, for example, several children who meet robots named Cog and Kismet. At times the robots appear to be engaged in conversation; at other times, the robots appear to be ignoring the children. The children respond to what they perceive about the robots and they tell stories about them. Turkle notes, "because Cog and Kismet cannot like or dislike, children's complicity is required to give the impression that there is an emerging fondness [between robot and child." In telling stories about these mechanized "people" the children include the robots in their circle. Turkle depicts a five-year-old who initially has difficulty getting Kismet to speak to her; when the robot finally does say something, the girl proclaims, "He trusts me."[33]

Significantly, Turkle finds an opposing direction happening in online discourse: exactly as people find themselves beginning to be drawn toward robots, they draw away from each other and from "real life" conversation and interaction. Online relationships intensify in often negative ways; even though people recognize that irony and sarcasm, for example, do not translate well in online communication, they will still attempt to be ironic. Invariably, this is misinterpreted; arguments escalate and people act in impolite and angry ways with each other, when often they would not get that angry offline.

More telling is how many people describe themselves as performing their identities online. They become more interactive, more outgoing, more able to disagree, than they would if they had a similar encounter offline. Turkle says, "Over time, such performances of identity may feel like identity itself."[34]

Some may be tempted to compare Turkle's sensibilities about identity performance to those of social reformers who suggest that we can revolt against the strictures of society by instigating new roles. After all, part of the mystique of the internet is that we are supposed to be able to construct our own identities in a revolutionary kind

---

[33] Sherry Turkle, *Alone Together: Why We Expect More From Technology and Less From Each Other* (New York: Basic Books, 2011). Kindle Edition, loc.1836.

[34] Sherry Turkle, Location 468.

of way. Some feminist scholars have often argued that gender (as opposed to the biologically based "sex"), usually known as a key trait in human identity, is socially constructed; the way to respond to social construction is through revolutionary tactics, to resist such gendered formulations in direct ways.[35] Yet postmodern scholar Judith Butler suggests that these roles are not so easily defeated, nor is the concept of sex devoid of socially constructed influences. The more we try to step "outside" what it means to be a woman or a man, the more social constructs ensnare us.[36] Her solutions rely instead on playing with the social roles – gender-bending, rather than on trying to leave behind "male" or "female."

When it comes to internet identity, it seems indeed that we cannot intelligibly create new identities. For example, many people use visual avatars when playing Massive Multiplayer Online Role-Playing Games (MMORPGs), including games like World of Warcraft and Second Life. Many times, people will choose avatars that are unlike themselves and then so see themselves as capable of acting in different ways. But studies on the effects of avatars are suggestive of unseen forces at work: "When researchers partially morph a person's face with a politician's, that person becomes more likely to approve of the politician—and has no clue why. As long as the ratio of the politician's features remains below 40 percent, the person doesn't even realize the photograph was doctored."[37] But moreover, the technology itself seems to be defeating any idea that we can intelligibly create distinctive online personas. Technologies like Kinect, which use 3-D avatars, enable people to "feel" like they are in rooms with other people, unlike with 2-D technologies such as video conferencing. Distinctions between being "online" or being physically "in a room with other people" become confused. To our technologized eyes, this is just fine – or even better than real life,

---

[35] This is seen, for example, in Judith Butler, *Gender Trouble*. (New York: Routledge Press, 1990).

[36] Judith Butler, *Bodies that Matter: On the Discursive Limits of Sex* (New York: Routledge, 1993).

[37] John Tierney, "3D Avatars Could Put You in Two Places at Once," *New York Times*, (April 11, 2011) http://www.nytimes.com/2011/04/12/science/12tier.html?_r=2&nl=todaysheadlines&emc=tha26. Accessed April 12, 2011. See also the study cited: Jeremy N. Bailenson, et al., "Facial Similarity Between Voters and Candidates Causes Influence" in *Public Opinion Quarterly*, 72.5: 935–61. http://poq.oxfordjournals.org/content/72/5/935.full. Accessed April 12, 2011.

for as journalist John Tierney notes, "The 3D avatar phenomenon enables people to interact with others in ways that are similar to real life interactions, only even 'better.'"[38]

Unlike the printing press, the internet enables forms of communication that make it difficult, if not impossible, to distinguish where the human and machine begin and end. Moreover, we who use these machines feel compelled to be with those machines constantly. "Always on, and (now) always with us, we tend the Net and the Net teaches us to need it," Turkle writes.[39] The technological class of humans experience themselves as always being "on the web" and always connected to machines that generate our experiences even as we believe we choose to participate. How many people are compelled to check all of their incoming text messages or emails? How many people think of their activities in terms of what can be Tweeted or posted on Facebook in such a way that makes a person able to portray themselves as they want to be seen?

This context puts the Lenten online fasts in different light. Even if these Christian online users are not recognizing themselves as cyborgs, they perceive a loss in themselves when they get too connected to the internet, and consequently disconnected from offline life. That loss is often displayed in bodily terms, such as being unable to bake bread or do other embodied activities. Perhaps they perceive themselves becoming too much the "machine."

The question and nature of embodiment becomes intensely important for these cyborgs who want to turn off. Unlike those who see that the internet fosters a mind/body dualism, in which the mind is permitted to be disembodied, the notion of the cyborg reminds us that it is a body that must use the computer, check the email, navigate the avatar, reflect on how to interact with these people online. At the most basic, fingers type, hands move mouses, eyes blink as they stare at the screens. Philosopher Hubert Dreyfus points out: "[I]f we were disembodied on the Internet, we wouldn't be able to acquire skills, we wouldn't be able to see what was relevant and not relevant, we wouldn't be able to relate to other people. So, the

---

[38] Ibid.

[39] Sherry Turkle, loc 3006.

Internet turns out to be a marvelous example of what we can and can't do without a body."[40]

In fact, when we consider the ways in which bodies use the internet, we may actually come to think that the internet is better for human bodies than television or the telephone. In those media, messages are very much two-dimensional with no ability for interaction. The internet, by contrast, allows for interaction with the medium itself, as well as with the many other bodies using the internet. The gravest mistake that can be made about the internet is that its users succumb to the fiction that only our minds are engaged, that we are disembodied, that there are no bodies on the other "end" of the conversation we might be having online.

Cyborg–human relationships

If the technological class is now unable to separate intelligibly from the web, what does that mean for humans' best visions if they could interact with each other on the web? As I have said, the story told about human identity online is that the web is a freeing, democratic space in which we could construct identities with boundlessness. In turn, our interactions with each other seemingly become boundless because the web appears to be a global place where we can interact with a variety of people in peaceable ways.

The conversations about *Avatar* mentioned above, however, might lead in other directions. Rather than seeing online lives (which, after all, are all avatar-based, as I mentioned above – an email address is a primitive avatar of a sort), the movie *Avatar* raises some questions about the limits of technology to create our identities and generate this ideal world of goodwill. James Cameron makes use of sophisticated technology to put on an avatar who is not white, not disabled, not a military veteran. On its face, this all seems good, until we see in the internet conversations mentioned above that perhaps all kinds of unhelpful constructs, including some about gender, race, and disability, end up being fostered by the very technologies that seek to overcome those divisions.

---

[40] "Interview with Hubert L. Dreyfus", *Conversations with History; Institute of International Studies*, UC Berkeley (2005). http://globetrotter.berkeley.edu/people5/Dreyfus/dreyfus-con7.html. Accessed April 12, 2011.

So it seems that just as postmodern scholars like Butler and Foucault have argued concerning gender, we cannot become revolutionary or idealistic on the web. For example, Eli Pariser, the first executive director of MoveOn.org, made a concerted effort to follow people online whose views differed from his own. He noticed that over time those voices started to disappear. Facebook and Google were curating the information he saw based on the "preferences" indicated by his clickstream. Pariser commented that the web "shows us what it thinks we need to see, but not what we should see."[41]

Another way to say this is to identify technology as political, meaning that technology can "embody specific forms of power and authority."[42] Langdon Winner identifies two ways in which technology is political. One way is that "specific features in the design or arrangement of a device or system could provide a convenient means of establishing patterns of power and authority. . .."[43] For instance, buildings that are not handicapped-accessible establish a kind of power over those who are wheelchair-bound. This first category of technologies demonstrates flexibility; people are able to bring about changes in these technologies, as people have done with advocating for wheelchair ramps. The second way is that there are "intractable properties of certain kinds of technology" linked to particular forms of authority. These technologies cannot be significantly changed to create differences in political structures, and there are no social systems (like capitalism or socialism) that could impact these intractable forms of technology. One example Winner gives is oil refineries: if refineries themselves are to operate efficiently, safely, and quickly, they necessitate a certain form of politics known as the modern hierarchical corporation.

Which form does the internet take? My use of Butler here gives me away; I think the internet fosters an intractable politic. In the next section, I briefly discuss what this means in relation to the

---

[41] Cited in Jennifer Cobb, "Can We Love the Stranger on Facebook", at *Being Blog*, (April 7, 2011), Krista Tippett, blog author, American Public Media, http://blog.onbeing.org/post/4413019671/can-we-love-the-stranger-on-facebook. Accessed May 26, 2011.

[42] Langdon Winner, *The Whale and the Reactor: A Search for Limits in an Age of High Technology* (Chicago, IL: University of Chicago Press, 1986), 19.

[43] Winner, 38.

strands of contemporary theological anthropology, especially those concerning race, class, gender, and disability identities.

Race and class

Cyborgs, it seems, are unable to construct nonracist worlds. For example, researcher danah boyd has studied teenagers for their uses of social networks. She noticed that there was a disparity between which social media teenagers used. African-American teens tended to log in to MySpace, but white teens logged in to Facebook. boyd notes:

> Teen preference for MySpace or Facebook went beyond simple consumer choice; it reflected a reproduction of social categories that exist in schools throughout the United States. Because race, ethnicity and socio-economic class shape social categories (Eckart, 1989), the choice between MySpace and Facebook became racialized. This got reinforced as teens chose to self-segregate across the two sites, just as they do in schools.[44]

boyd compares the "white flight" to the suburbs with the "flight" to Facebook (which had more affluent users than MySpace) as a way of naming the racial and class disparities she was seeing.

More disturbing is the way some internet platforms are used to subjugate people and redescribe real-life racial tensions. Lisa Namakura, for example, discusses the phenomenon of "gold farming," playing a MMORPG to gain in-game currency and then sell it to other players. No one knows for sure how many gold farmers exist, nor where the largest trafficking points are, but officials often note China and Korea as two key sites. Namakura notes that online players use Asian stereotypes to ridicule players they presume to be gold farmers.[45] *The Guardian* newspaper made such charges about online racism worse when it reported in 2011

---

[44] danah boyd, "White Flight in Networked Publics? How Race and Class Shaped American Teen Engagement with MySpace and Facebook," in Race after the Internet. Lisa Nakamura and Peter Chow-White, eds. New York: Routledge, 2011: 203–22.

[45] Lisa Nakamura, "Don't Hate the Player, Hate the Game: The Racialization of Labor in World of Warcraft," *Critical Studies in Media Communication*, 26.2 (June 2009): 128–44.

about prison guards in China exploiting real-life prisoners by forcing them to play online games to earn virtual money.

Interestingly, at the same time that such activities happen online, Facebook draws another charge, of being too genteel. Vanessa Grigoriadis uses the language of nineteenth-century houses to describe the changes she sees in the internet. The internet of old was like the Wild West, the "new frontier." In the supposed "old internet" with its "new frontier" mentality, people could perhaps presume the kind of boundlessness that is associated with online identity.[46] That metaphor is quickly being swept aside on Facebook, with its privacy rules and its denotations of who are friends, who are members of one's groups and the like:

> Now online life is a series of Victorian drawing rooms, a well-tended garden where you bring your calling card and make polite conversation with those of your kind, a sanitized city on a hill where amity reigns. . . . We prepare our faces, then come and go, sharing little bits of data, like photos, haikus, snippets of conversations—the intellectual property that composes our lives.[47]

The new spaces of the internet are more composed; as Eli Pariser says, it is difficult even to find the "other," those who are different from ourselves, because our interactions with other is limited by the medium of the web. We do not seek out others, our minds do not become broadened.

Gender

Anecdotally, I find that my writing a book such as this one puts me in a minority of people writing on this topic. When I have presented some of these chapters at conferences, I have frequently found myself the only woman in the room, save perhaps the moderator. Adrian

---

[46] I am suspicious, though, of an overidealized version of the internet as "new frontier" as well.

[47] Vanessa Grigoriadis, "Do You Own Facebook or Does Facebook Own You?" in *New York Times Magazine*, (April 5, 2009) http://nymag.com/news/features/55878/. Accessed April 19, 2011.

Rorty presents an argument that may account for this disparity: men create technology for women to use. He examines the rise and development of home furnishings, for example, noting that the nineteenth century was a time when women were expected to make use of the various textiles and other goods produced by men, in order to furnish a home entirely distinct from the workplace.[48] So perhaps, men get to theorize about the internet while women use it? For it is very clear that many, many women make use of the internet and call it their community. So Mora Aarons Mele asks:

> Does a nation of mommybloggers and giggling girls on MySpace also reinforce traditional gender stereotypes? We're comfortable with women being outspoken on matters close to home. But while plenty of women bloggers write with intelligence and wit about everything from the economic crisis to foreign policy, they get rewarded (with advertiser money or media coverage) when they do stick closer to home.[49]

The phenomenon of gender-swapping provides another avenue for considering the extent to which people really can "fight the system." When researchers asked about gender swapping, they found many reasons why this might occur, the answers were telling. "Mostly my characters are female, but I think I made my male character because I was tired of creepy guys hitting on my female characters. It's utterly ridiculous, very annoying, and not the reason why I play the game. (P39, female, age 32)"[50] Or: "I mostly play female characters, but sometimes I make a male character and don't let anyone know I'm female in real life. It's interesting how different people treat you when they think you are male. . . . (P117, female, age 23)"[51] And, "If you play a chick and know what the usual nerd wants to read, you

---

[48] Elsie deWolf, *The House in Good Taste* (New York: 1913), cited in Adrian Rorty, *Objects of Desire: Design and Society 1750–1980* (London: Cameron Books, 1986), 104.

[49] Morra Aarons Mele, "Exploring the Gendered Web," *Gender and Technology: Berkman Center for Internet and Society*, (April 17, 2009) http://blogs.law.harvard.edu/genderandtech/tag/facebook/. Accessed April 19, 2011.

[50] Zaheer Hussain and Mark Griffiths, "Gender Swapping and Socializing in Cyberspace: An Exploratory Study," in *CyberPsychology and Behavior*, 11.1 (2008): 47–53, 50.

[51] Ibid.

will get free items. . . which in turn I pass them to my other male characters. . . very simple. Nerd + Boob = Loot. (P65, male, age 20)" Though all of these commenters have slightly different reasons for swapping genders, they all also suggest that there is a fixed nature to being a man or a woman online. Women are sex objects; men get treated "differently." Cyborgs do not apparently even have the grace to pretend they are not thinking about women in lustful ways, as often happens offline by contemporary social norms.

Disability

Disability may be the one area where being a cyborg rids divides between people. In fact, "cyborg" is the term Deaf people use to refer to having cochlear implants, another kind of technology to which people are always connected.[52] In past decades before the rise of the web, such an identity might make one see Deaf people as not quite human; in a world where we are human but indistinguishable from our machine-tools, perhaps such a dehumanizing view does not exist.

Perhaps this is the case, but I am sure that as with other ways cyborgs are able to perpetuate distance between themselves and others, so will this work in disability. For example, in her work on sociable robotics, Sherry Turkle says that people often envision robots for the elderly and those with disabilities.[53] So, it is exactly those populations that are already marginalized in our culture that now seem deserving of robots who cannot "humanly care" for a person, even if the robots are capable of enacting certain caring procedures, like giving baths or transporting patients.

The myth of meeting the other

What does it mean to consider ourselves as cyborgs, at least for those humans who exhibit the kind of connectivity of which I speak? Part of naming a group as cyborgs is to recognize the very different life that heavy internet users have compared with many others. MsDerious'

---

[52] See, for example, James Cherney's article "Deaf Culture and the Cochlear Implant Debate: Cyborg Politics and the Identity of People with Disabilities," in *Argumentation and Advocacy,* 36(1), (Summer 1999): 22–34.

[53] Sherry Turkle, loc. 2222.

comment pinpoints exactly that now "cyborg" becomes another way of dividing the world. Now we do not merely have the "haves" and "have nots" – there are humans, and there are cyborgs, and cyborgs tend to be the ones with power and information. This power becomes even more marked because of the internet's myth of being boundless.

Part of naming us as cyborgs is that it makes sense of how we can perceive the internet as being a boundless space and yet be unaware of how the spaces, and peoples, are quite bounded. We carry the problems our "real-life" society faces into our online interactions. As it has turned out, the idea that the internet would make us free to form other identities turns out not to be the case. Racism still exists online and sexism still exists, and perhaps in more virulent forms.

It turns out that what we imagined about the internet – that it would be an open, interactive place where the concept of identity gets turned on its head – is, in fact, limited by our offline world. A cyborg may be a human attached to web-based technology (in particular), but contrary to science fiction or movies like *The Matrix*, the cyborg does not thereby gain a grander, more knowledgeable view of the world. While there is a significant minority of people who find internet identity to be freeing, it is not the preferred mode of relating: in one study, only twenty percent of the people studied thought that online interaction was more satisfying than offline interaction.[54] Other researchers have found that people use the internet to maintain offline relationships,[55] a fact which is not necessarily helpful, as this is probably one of the reasons why the offline world becomes mirrored in the online world.[56]

Can cyborg be saved?

As often happens in discussions about theological anthropology, this chapter has become more about humanity and what they are becoming, than it has been about God. In conclusion, I return to

---

[54] Hussain and Griffiths, 51.

[55] Hussain and Griffiths, Ibid.

[56] Helena Cole and Mark Griffiths, "Social Interactions in Massively Multiplayer Online Role-Playing Gamers," in *CyberPsychology and Behavior*, 10.4 (2007): 575–83, 581.

the poignant comments about a Lenten fast. "Turning off" reflects, for some commenters, a nagging suspicion that God cannot meet them online. Perhaps this is because Cyborg seems to be a wholly human invention that, conversely, makes us less human. What Thomas Aquinas knew about God as the source no longer makes sense, unless we disconnect. But in addition, the concern with being cyborgs online is that "when we employ the latest generation of Web tools, we lose some control over the message. . . ,"[57] especially the gospel message. Christians are unable clearly to communicate who God in Christ *is* in Web 2.0 formats because the collaborative nature of Web 2.0 means that any message can be edited at any time. Confusion happens in internet communities because of the lack of nuance that image-based communication involves. Even God no longer makes sense to the social cyborg.

Our salvation therefore apparently comes in disconnecting and in practicing baking bread and dancing and all the offline things that make us not machine. Perhaps this is, indeed, the direction we must go. I am not convinced, however, partly because I argued in the previous chapter that God is, in fact, online. But moreover, I am not convinced that we can "turn off" quite that easily. Nor that the main way we social cyborgs can find salvation from our technological selves (and the racism and sexism and other isms that are still, to probable dismay, present online) is to disengage. This is not to say that "fasting" from the internet isn't a good practice; quite the contrary. But as I suggested in Chapter 2, God is involved in and part of our lives as humans, and we humans are always inextricably part of both the earthly city and the City of God. The internet provides neither a haven from that fact, nor does it wholly promote an earthly city over a godly one. Becoming social cyborgs does not negate God's encounters with our lives. Being social cyborgs merely shows, once again, that an inextricable facet of human life is that we are changeable creatures, in part because of our desires for technology.

What are we Christian cyborgs to be, then? How do we witness God to the world in which we find ourselves? In the next three chapters I explore this further. In Chapter 4, I consider the internet as one of the Powers that can possibly be "tamed," building on

---

[57] Kallenberg, 78.

the discussion of power I mention above. In Chapter 5, I consider what kinds of online communities we might want to be part of, if we wish to tame its power and witness to God well on the internet. And in Chapter 6, I more fully contemplate ethics – the specific ways internet theologians engage each other online and what their collective wisdom might say about engaging the internet.

4

Empowering power: Scripture, authority, and sources in Web 2.0 theology

Comment at a Catholic discussion board on appropriate sources to use

The Catechism of the Catholic Church is a good start. After that, the Code of Canon Law, and for the Liturgy, the [General Instruction on the Roman Missal]. Otherwise, people tend to just go on their gut feelings, and that's how we end up with the mess we have now.[1]

Devin Rose, "Ask a Catholic. . ."

With the advent of the internet, accurate information is now accessible to anyone who wants to find it.[2]

---

[1] PonyExpress2, Comment in "Duggar Announcement," *Natural Family Planning Discussion Board*, (June 21, 2011) http://forums.delphiforums.com/nfptalk/messages?msg=147078.1290. Accessed Junc 22, 2011.

[2] Devin Rose, "Ask a Catholic. . . . (Devin Responds) at *Rachel Held Evans Author Speaker Blogger*, (July 12, 2011) http://rachelheldevans.com/ask-a-catholic-response. Accessed July 12, 2011.

The internet conversation: A power that deceives?

Thus far, I have discussed the idea that the internet is created and that human beings interact with this creation in mixed ways. In this chapter, I bring these concerns together to think about the internet as one of the scriptural Powers and Principalities. Paul speaks of the Powers several times in the New Testament. In his letter to the Colossians, he discusses Jesus Christ in relation to the Powers: "He is the image of the invisible God, the firstborn of all creation; for in him all things in heaven and on earth were created, things visible and invisible, whether thrones or dominions or rulers or powers— all things have been created through him and for him."[3] Further, in Romans 8:38–39, he writes: "For I am convinced that neither death, nor life, nor angels, nor rulers, nor things present, nor things to come, nor powers, nor height, nor depth, nor anything else in all creation, will be able to separate us from the love of God in Christ Jesus our Lord."[4] But what exactly are these Powers?

Several theologians, especially in Protestant contexts, have investigated the Powers over the past few decades and have seen that the Powers and Principalities name structures that are integral to human life. For example, Biblical scholar John Howard Yoder names some of the kinds of Powers to which scripture refers: "intellectual structures (-ologies and –isms) moral structures (codes and customs), political structures (the tyrant, the market, the school, the courts, race and nation). The totality is overwhelmingly broad."[5] Yoder goes on to affirm that God created the world and all that is in it as good, including these Powers. "There could not be society or history, there could not be humanity without the existence above us of religious, intellectual, moral, and social structures."[6] And yet, says Yoder, one of the truths of the world as that these Powers "fail to serve us as they should. They do not enable humanity to live a genuinely free, loving life."[7]

---

[3] Col. 1:15–16, NRSV.

[4] NRSV.

[5] John Howard Yoder, *The Politics of Jesus*, Second Edition (Grand Rapids, MI: Eerdmans Publishing Company, 1994), 143.

[6] Ibid.

[7] Ibid.

In this chapter, I claim that seeing the internet as a Power is an apt way for thinking about Christian engagement with online life. I explore some of the ways the internet does not "enable humanity to live a genuinely free, loving life" by considering the online theological conversations about authority. In scripture, authority (the Greek word *exousiai)* goes along with power, especially by considering God's authority and power.[8] The scriptures also note that the Powers often have certain kinds of authority over human beings in contrast to God's authority. So, by discussing the ways of authority online, I seek to "unmask" the Power of the internet[9] and show it in contrast to God's authority. In so doing, I hope to enable Christians to think better about how to use the internet and not allow it to be merely a tool, or wholly good, or wholly bad.

First, I look at internet discussion on online authority. I discuss authority in relation to both Catholic and Protestant concerns, for these do show up differently, at times. This discussion about authority in turn raises questions about the extent to which the internet is a broadly democratic freeing space, open to a range of ideas that supposedly allows for better and broader conversation. Following this look at online discussions of, and uses of, authority, I then more fully discuss the way in which the internet might be a Power, drawing on others' discussions of the Powers and how they operate. My conclusion in this chapter is that internet theologians need to recognize the internet as a Power so that they can then learn rightly how to relate to it.

Catholics and the magisterium

To begin with, the quotes that I mention at the beginning of this chapter tell two different versions of sources online. The first, from the Catholic discussion board, is mentioned in discussion of the Catholic Church's teachings against artificial contraception. The

---

[8] Marva Dawn, *Powers, Weakness, and the Tabernacling of God* Kindle Edition (Grand Rapids, MI: Eerdmans, 2001), Chapter 1.

[9] "Unmasking" the Powers is one of the themes in Walter Wink's several works on the Powers. See especially the second volume of his trilogy, *Unmasking the Powers: The Invisible Forces that Determine Human Existence* (Philadelphia, PA: Fortress Press, 1986).

discussion thread began as a discussion of the Duggar family, which has become famous through the TLC show "Nineteen Kids and Counting." The show depicts various experiences of the family as they navigate raising nineteenth children ranging in age from baby- and toddlerhood to young adulthood. The discussion thread initially focused on family size but veered, however, to discussions of "providentialism" and the Quiverfull movement, both practices by some Christian groups where couples eschew using birth control, instead relying on God's "providence." The conversation then became more squarely Catholic, as members discussed the Catholic Church's teachings against artificial contraception, which in turn led to wondering what God's will is for people and how would we know?

In that context, Ponyexpress2 suggests that internet conversations seem just to be a free-for-all so that those who wish to discuss theology online or find religiously minded groups will quickly find themselves in a "mess" where everyone goes with their "gut." The author of the comment is replying to another poster who expresses concern about knowing "what is right when it doesn't seem right to anyone else" especially in relation to salvation. Neither of the posters wants to do something that would lead to "eternal damnation" so in the face of the internet's apparent unrelenting open-endedness, they seek concrete, authoritative sources for thinking theologically. Thus, PonyExpress2 advocates for the Catechism, Canon Law, and encyclicals as "authoritative." Other voices may swirl around, claiming other views, but these will remain as authoritative sources for Catholic web users. One of the difficulties, however, with trying to maintain a discrete list such as this one is that it is incomplete, especially against the backdrop of the entire Catholic tradition. There is great potential, therefore, to limit theological conversations in troublesome ways by trying to generate such a list, even as the opposite problem of having no authorities at all also exists. What about *scripture*, without which it is hard to imagine understanding God in Christ, the church, the sacraments, or any number of other things? What about the lives of the saints? What about theological reflection done by well-respected theologians across the centuries?

By contrast, Catholic convert Devin Rose, a lay apologist, blogger, and author of *If Protestantism is True*, finds the internet to be a source of "accurate information" without naming specific sources. Rose's statement is suggestive of the Wikipedia ideal of knowledge, which is that collectively, we have better information than any individual, even any one expert, can have. Rose is answering questions put to him at Rachel Held Evans' blog, where he was asked to be a guest poster, explaining Catholicism to Evans' largely Protestant audience. One of the questions Rose is asked to address is: "What would you say is most misunderstood about the Roman Catholic Church? And what are some of the strangest questions you have received from Protestants about your faith?"[10] Part of Rose's response is to suggest to Protestants:

> The gospel gets boiled down to the belief that man is justified through the imputed alien righteousness of Christ, and if you don't think that is accurate, you must not be a Christian. So I would encourage you to go deeper. Cut through the FUD [fear, uncertainty, doubt]. Examine the issues you find problematic and see what the Catholic Church really teaches about them and why. The answers may surprise you.

Moreover, the answers are available online, and Rose does not delineate where those answers may be found. He leaves it up to the individual internet users to find the appropriate sources that give the answers, though he does give his own hints throughout his answers, via links to Vatican websites or other sources that he himself sees as authoritative.

These two authors display one of the important facets of online discourse: the link, and especially, the good link. Links become good for citation on the internet: if it exists in a link, then whatever idea the link is used to support has some kind of substantiation. There is a kind of hierarchy of links, which can be found by examining "search engine optimization" sites that help businesses and others market their websites. These marketing sites know that certain links have more authority, and therefore more visitors, than other links, based in part on the order in which a web page appears after an online search is conducted.

One marketing firm found that the lowest level of authority of links are "free blogs and forums"; at the middle level include "higher quality" sites like Twitter and web pages that have RSS feeds or blog

---

[10] Rose, http://rachelheldevans.com/ask-a-catholic-response.

rolls. Web pages (and therefore links) with the highest authority come federal .gov and higher education .edu sites. Worldwide directories (like Yahoo) and web pages have "a significant quantity of links pointing to it."[11] Note that while in some cases, the link's relative importance is connected to an offline institution that tends to be viewed as authoritative (i.e. the government is seen as a reliable source for statistics), many sources of authority result solely in relation to online interactions, such as whether a blogger has an RSS feed on their blog, or whether others have linked to a blog. Internet users therefore tend to construct authoritative links by their very activity online. The difficulty is that if an authoritative link is authoritative because of the number of people linking to it, internet users are merely reinforcing the authority already established online when they link the same link as their friends.

Theologians Anthony Godzieba and Vincent Miller help further make clear how a seemingly open-ended medium such as this one could limit theological conversation online. Both are Roman Catholic theologians considering the Church's authority in the new web-based contexts in which we find ourselves, which has become even more important since Pope Benedict XVI has emphasized the need for priests and lay people to be witnesses on the internet.

Godzieba argues that new media spaces, exemplified by the internet, do not respect traditional boundaries of the magisterium. It is key to note that for Godzieba, the magisterium prior to the internet age is not how some Catholics would describe it, as the pope and his bishops, but the whole two-thousand-year tradition, tested and conditioned by time and space and tradition. On Godzieba's view, when one looks across that broad swath of history, one small statement made by a bishop mattered little at first, but picked up authority over time. By contrast, Godzieba discusses how magisterial statements are viewed today: he marvels how minor statements that have low magisterial status are "granted near-absolute, 'deal-clinching' status," especially by academic theologians.[12] Godzieba's

---

[11] DenverSeoMarketing.com, "Determining Link Value and Relative Value," (No date) http://www.denverseomarketing.com/Link-Hierarchy.htm. Accessed September 19, 2011.

[12] Anthony Godzieba, "Quaestio Disputata: The Magisterium in an Age of Digital Reproduction," in When the Magisterium Intervenes (Collegeville: The Liturgical Press, forthcoming 2012).

example centers on some minor, very offhand statements John Paul II made about the vegetative state and how that one minor statement made it into major works by prominent ethicists. How did this happen? Godzieba argues that it is the digital form, the fact that the pope's comments were available immediately on the internet that determined the remark's importance.

From Godzieba's point of view, the effect of the internet is that authority becomes centralized to the point that the church mimics a corporation, with the Pope as CEO, rather than the "dynamic, historically-situated view of *communio* rooted in the patristic period and retrieved by twentieth-century Catholic ecclesiology."[13] Godzieba's solution is for theologians to be counter-cultural and to live deeply embodied lives that counter act the influence of the digital age.

Vincent Miller finds Godzieba's account to be somewhat incomplete, as it does not take into account that even while authority seems to be centralized, that authority is also eroding due to the effects of digital immediacy. In concert with this are the effects of technological advance and consumer culture, which lead on the one hand to "heterogenization" – the fact that more and more communities of people exist on the internet, which makes the internet more and more diverse – and on the other hand, "deterritorialization," the fact that these diverse communities no longer have to interact with each other directly in the internet medium.

The result of both heterogenization and deterritorialization is that they lead to more sectarian movements and ever more homogeneous groups of people. Miller suggests: "constructing a shared identity in such an undifferentiated, deterritorialized setting favors elements of religious traditions and practices which elicit strong emotions or set a community apart from others. Attachment to tradition may remain strong, but it is not practiced in a comprehensive manner. Rather, elements are lifted from it that sustain a clear identity."[14] PonyExpress2 provides a very neat example of Miller's point in her insistence about the "right" Catholic sources, which were simply

---

[13] Godzieba, 11.

[14] Vincent J. Miller, "When Mediating Structures Change: Transformations of Magisterial Authority in Digital Culture," in *When the Magisterium Intervenes* (Collegeville: The Liturgical Press, forthcoming 2012).

a few online links removed from their contexts. It is curious, for example, that PonyExpress2 mentions canon law, a highly technical field. Canon lawyers have debates about the nuances of the law, but in this discussion, canon law seems safely solid.

Miller names groups like the Catholic discussion board discussed above as "special agenda organizations" (borrowing from Robert Wuthnow) and sees them as the ways by which people are reached in an age where theological conversation happens on the internet. The most effective bishops, the most effective voices of the magisterium, Miller argues, are not relying on their magisterial roles alone, but make use of special agenda organizations to make their message. Miller's example is Archbishop Chaput, whose discussing of voting in the 2008 election spread widely beyond the borders of his archdiocese because several special interest groups found his message to be more congenial than the messages from their own respective bishops.[15] The result, however, is that conversation becomes limited to the interests of the special agenda group and the nuances of the conversations are eliminated. In the example of the election, Miller notes how painstakingly the US Council of Bishops had noted that respect-for-life issues as well as social justice questions had to be accounted for when it came time to vote. Abortion was to be given some consideration but not to the exclusion of absolutely every other issue. Special interest groups, however, removed the nuances of the bishops' statement and made the question solely about abortion.

Protestants and scripture

Catholic conversation is often concerned with authority in relation to the church's magisterium, which Protestants might readily dismiss. Consider, however, the ways in which the authority of scripture becomes reconfigured online. For example, an offline reader might take a look at a Bible and say that these are the scriptures; these are authoritative. Online, however, Biblical authority takes on a different tone. Do a Google search of Philippians 2, for example, and the link hierarchy is displayed. Biblegateway.com garners the first two links, where one can find either the New International

---

[15] Miller, 13.

Standard version, or the King James Version. Third on the page is the English Standard Version, with its own website, www.esvbible. org aimed at Christians who use (or used to use) the King James Version of the Bible, for the site comes with a note of apology and "respect" to the King James Version of the Bible. Searchers would likely not notice, for example, the New Revised Standard Version (a favorite of many academic scholars), which is located at the very bottom of the first screen.

More than that, though, scriptures are now being read in ways far different from how Christians have read in the past. Ched Spellman writes, "A digitized and destabilized Bible exists in a different way than in a physical codex form. . . .When reading the Bible online or on a mobile device, most of the time there will be rival texts vying for the attention and focus of the reader."[16] These rival texts are not usually other parts of scripture, as they would have been for readers of the Bible-as-book, who could flip between different chapters or books to compare texts. Instead, hyperlinks can link readily to other sources, and social media sites enable scriptures to be read alongside numerous other things:

> [T]he proverb of the day might appear right below your nephew's birthday pictures, that bit of commentary on the book of Revelation comes just above your friend from high school's comments on the season finale of LOST, and the Psalm you read a few moments ago gets buried in the Facebook feed just as quick as the embedded You Tube video that played while you were reading it.[17]

Similarly, an NPR essay suggests that we now take in more information by small bites, rather than reading a whole book.[18] Snippets mean more than the completion of a whole book, even if the book's plot was beautifully conceived and constructed. Some might complain that this fosters a lack of nuance and complexity, but on

---

[16] Ched Spellman, "The Canon After Google: Implications of a Digitized and Destabilized Codex," *Princeton Theological Review* XVII.2 (Fall 2010): 39–42, 41.

[17] Ibid.

[18] Linton Weeks, "We Are Just Not Digging the Whole Anymore," *NPR* online (March 15,2011)http://www.npr.org/2011/03/15/134531653/we-are-just-not-digging-the-whole-anymore. Accessed March 15, 2011.

another view, amassing bits and pieces means that more complexity
is possible. Rather than reading a few whole books by, say, ten
authors, we can compile several tidbits from a hundred or more
authors. What this does mean is that someone is not learning how
to do deep reflective thinking with those few authors but it doesn't
necessarily mean that we are not doing deep reflective thinking.
Scripture reading becomes more scattered than it was before.
Once, the danger was proof-texting, using snippets of scripture
out of context of the whole story. Now the danger is that scripture
appears as just one more flexible, moveable authority online. Like
the Catholic commenters I mentioned above, Protestants may very
well find themselves trying to grasp the links and sites that are most
authoritative in the fluidity of the internet.

Shane Hipps writes also about the case of the disappearing Bible.
He is one of the many who see a parallel between the advent of
the printing press and the advent of the internet. He argues that
the advent of the printing press allowed for books, which in turn
promoted a "left-brain" culture, which in turn provided a way for
Protestants to defy the authority of the pope. Internet cultures,
however, are shrinking even the Protestant authority of scripture.
"Consider blogs. . . . Blogs are ill-suited for deep-level analysis and
thoughtful reasoning. The Internet makes a flat stone of the mind
and skips it across the surface of the world's information ocean."[19]
This makes the authority of the Bible of no more consequence than
someone's blog.

Alongside the question of scripture as authoritative, internet
theologians raise questions about pastoral authority. Theologian and
Pastor Justin Bailey, also a blogger, writes, "To the question, 'Who
holds the truth?' bloggers answer: 'We do – all of us.'"[20] Though
Bailey himself is a pastor, he seems to be undermining his own
authority as clergy to describe, instead, the authority of "all of us"
Christians online. Bailey further suggests that the internet enables
us to choose "which products to buy, whose information to believe,
and whose truth to live. . ."[21] Freedom, as well as democracy, is a

---

[19] Shane Hipps, *Flickering Pixels* (Grand Rapids, MI: Zondervan Press, 2009), 146.

[20] Justin A. Bailey, "Welcome to the Blogosphere," in *Everyday Theology: How to Read Cultural Texts and Interpret Trends*, Kevin Vanhoozer, ed (Grand Rapids, MI: Baker Academic Press, 2007), 181.

[21] Bailey, 181.

mark of Bailey's discourse.[22] Bloggers practice this kind of discourse among a community of people who comment and critique their thought, so that each internet user provides a sounding board for other users.

Bailey then makes a crucial theological link: "a community of trustworthy interpreters: that sounds a bit like a church, doesn't it?"[23] But if bloggers are changing the way church is done online, Bailey also sees that authority must be changing as well. He writes, "If authority is being taken from the hands of the 'sanctioned authorities' and placed in the hands of the public, could this mean that the authority structure of the church is changing as well?"[24] Another blogger, Tim Bednar, writes an essay on blogging and the cyberchurch that is notably named "We Know More than Our Pastors." Bednar argues that bloggers have better Christian practices and know more about how to witness to the people of today than traditional pastors of brick-and-mortar congregations. He thereby suggests that whatever authority churches have is more likely being set adrift from the moorings of the traditional church settings and hierarchies with which it had been associated.

In addition, this democratic and open society is given quite high status for those who see the internet as mostly a force for good because it allows for a range of viewpoints and ultimately, people, to find a voice, a community, a set of people who support them. On this view, the internet feeds into the ideas that political liberalism has set forth since the eighteenth century and that have solidified in particular ways in the late twentieth century. For example, the internet appears to support individuals seeking their own self-fulfillment

---

[22] The recent Wikileaks scandal manifested several questions about authority, for example. Not only was there the authority of the various states mentioned in the Wikileaks documents particularly on businesses like Amazon and Mastercard, but there was also a clamor on the internet, directed precisely toward those governments that purport to be democratic, that arresting the Wikileaks founder was hypocritical to democracy. Washington Post commentator Tim Hwang discussed Wikileaks as a "Long War"; one side is the army of decentralization and open internet space; the other side is the army of corporations and political regimes who want to control internet space. See Tim Hwang, "Wikileaks and the Internet's Long War," *Washington Post Online* (December 12, 2010) http://www.washingtonpost.com/wp-dyn/content/article/2010/12/10/AR2010121002604.html. Accessed February 24, 2011.

[23] Bailey, 182.

[24] Bailey, 183.

and happiness, and it perpetuates a society that appears to enable
every individual to be truly herself, supported by an open, broad
community. Authority goes only so far as each individual determines
for himself; the internet merely offers an array of choices for an
individual to use.

There is a bug in the works, however, which is the extent to
which internet communities either support or enable their members
to be happy and fulfilled, because the internet is not set up to make
its users reflective about what it means to be human, or to be happy
or fulfilled. This is an issue that medical ethicist Carl Elliot mentions
in his book *Better than Well.* He knows that medically there are
people who do not feel normal if they have all of their limbs and
that these apotemnophiliacs seek surgeons willing to cut off their
limbs. Elliot notes that these "amputees by choice," who comprise a
very tiny portion of the population, would not have found a voice
or a community of like-minded individuals except for the fact that
the internet exists and connects solitary people across the world
into an actual group.[25]

Before the almost limitless space of the internet existed, people
separated by geography had no way to know that there were others
"like them." That other members of the group validate amputees'
choices to amputate, in ways that the "general" community at large
would not, and it potentially enables people to be truly "themselves"
because they are able to reframe themselves as not-odd. To Elliot's
own surprise as a medical researcher, he finds himself having some
sympathy with these amputees. After all, what is it, really, that
makes their decisions rationally any different from people who
decide to have plastic surgery or undertake any number of other
"personal enhancements" designed to help a person feel more "like
themselves"?

It is due to the internet, however, that apotemnophilia is exactly
un-like plastic surgery, for plastic surgery is able to play in the
world of print media and television. While there are communities
dedicated to helping people deal with plastic surgery online, plastic
surgery does not get its validation and sanctification from online
activities and neither do the people who have plastic surgery
done. It is only via the internet, however, that apotemnophilia has

[25] Carl Elliot, *Better Than Well: American Medicine Meets the American Dream* (New
York: W.W. Norton & Company, 2003), Chapter 9.

standing. But it is also the internet that is decidedly unable to help either medical doctors or apotemnophiliacs themselves reflect on whether it is healthy to desire to lose an arm. The fact that the internet merely allows for people to group together, without at the same time fostering ways for those people to reflect on their activity and think through whether it is humanizing or not, is a serious problem.

Another example of this might well be pornography use online. According to Ogi Ogas, co-author of *A Billion Wicked Thoughts*, porn sites make up about four percent of total website space online, but about thirteen percent of online searches. About 2.5% of all internet users go online to one adult site LiveJasmin each month, a rather high use of one site![26] So internet users are free to view and use porn online. Questions about how easy access to porn influences how we understand our bodies and our relationships remain, however. Structurally, the internet is not equipped to help its users think through these questions.

Moreover, the story that there is little or no authority, except for oneself, turns out not to be very true. In the Web 2.0 world, there are actually some clear delineations of authority, contrary to what Justin Bailey suggests. Some bloggers and tweeters have authority and some do not. The determination of authority relates in part to how often and regularly a person posts, and how good their writing is. Ultimately, however, authority resides principally in the question of how many people are reading your blog or tweets. Large numbers of viewers presume that the blogger in question usually has something important or worthwhile to say, but numbers are not the only marker of authority. Even more important than the number of views are the number of comments and the ability of a blog to appear on a Google website.[27] These facts give lie to the idea that Web 2.0 is quite so totally the boundless, democratic medium, (open to all, so that all have an equal voice and that authority is spread over the totality of people) that Bailey and others depict.

There is hierarchy in blogdom and twitterdom; newbies have to learn how to play by the rules or their posting and questions will

---

[26] Ogi Ogas and Sai Gaddam, *A Billion Wicked Thoughts* (New York: Penguin, 2011).

[27] See, for example, Darren Rowse, "How to Build Blog Authority -Technorati Style," *ProBlogger*, (November 8, 2006) http://www.problogger.net/archives/2006/11/08/how-to-build-blog-authority-technorati-style. Accessed January 4, 2010.

be ignored. Indeed, Bednar himself opines that very few blogs make it past the two-month mark, which he mentions disparagingly; in his words, blogging is a "spiritual discipline," and he discusses that the cyberchurch is a rather small, niche community. He writes, "we desire to find the 'truth' not as isolated individuals, who get revelations directly from God, instead we believe the truest truth is found collectively." Yet, the collective is not large enough to encompass those who are not members of the blogging community – that is, the rest of Christendom. Truth, here, is available only to a small few online.

Brett McCracken, author of *Hipster Christianity: When Church and Cool Collide*,[28] observes:

> Some would suggest that one of the values in the church embracing the networked paradigm of social media technology is that it allows for a broader, more diverse connectedness. It allows the connecting pockets and nodes of local church communities to be bound together across great distances. In this situation, the church becomes decentralized and flattened, a community of equals in which *authority comes not from individuals but from the collective*. It is the Wikipedia model of cooperative truth-telling and collective intelligence – the notion that a self-correcting network will over time become a more reliable source than any one person or institution, regardless of resources.[29]

McCracken worries, though: Is this flattened collective really what the church is meant to be? Is this view of authority as coming from everywhere really forming disciples of Christ, or is it, as he suspects, fostering "pride and narcissism"?[30]

When it comes to authority and the internet, then, I find that the Catholics who maintained that there were only a few links that were trustworthy, and the Christians who think that the internet is

---

[28] Brett McCracken, *Hipster Christianity: When Church and Cool Collide* (Chicago, IL: Baker Books, 2010).

[29] Brett McCracken, "The Separation of Church and Status: How Online Social Networking Helps and Hurts the Church," *Princeton Theological Review* XVII.2 (Fall 2010): 21–34, 31. Available online at http://www.princetontheologicalreview. org/issues_pdf/43.pdf. Emphasis mine.

[30] Ibid., 33.

an open space that allows for free trade in truth, are operating on similar principles because both are trying to respond to the idea of the internet as an open, democratic space that appears not to be authoritative. Yet, there is authority online, regardless of whether one tries to neatly package that authority into two or three reliable sites or tries to suggest that there is no authority. Either way, the internet conceals its power from us, and so we must learn to see the internet in different and better ways.

The power of the internet

I have tried, thus far, to expose some of the ways in which the internet has authority and power in human life. This is part of the reason I want to name the internet as one of the Powers and Principalities, for I am also suggesting that the internet is one of many social structures which affects our ability to follow Jesus well. In saying so, I am arguing against those Christians who want to see following Jesus simply as a matter of individual expression of faith over against everything else in the world. While an individual's faith is important, it is also important to see that the world affects discipleship positively and negatively. The internet influences people to act in ways that are not necessarily Christ-like.

To make the claim that the internet exists as one of the Powers is to say that the internet is part of God's creation, but that it is fallen. Theologian Charles Pinches writes, "The powers order human life, and so make a certain form of it possible. However, they also distort, since they are tempted to overreach and become idolatrous."[31]

Scriptures affirm that the Powers are created: "For in him all things in heaven and on earth were created, things visible and invisible, whether thrones or dominions or rulers or powers—all things have been created through him and for him."[32] John Howard Yoder advises Christians to remember that since the Powers are created, we also acknowledge that they had some kind of goodness: "Society and history, even nature, would be impossible

---

[31] Charles Pinches, "Hauerwas and Political Theology: The Next Generation," *Journal of Religious Ethics* 36.3 (2008): 513 42, 528.

[32] Colossians 1:16, NRSV.

without regularity, system, and order – and God has provided for this need."[33] The internet makes certain versions of life possible, especially for people who have never been without its technology. Many people these days cannot fathom how to drive from one place to another without using MapQuest or Google Maps, nor how to obtain encyclopedic information without using search engines, nor how to stay connected with friends without the use of Twitter and Facebook.

In acknowledging the creatureliness of the Powers, we acknowledge that there is no object outside God's purview. So, the internet must also be understood as part of God's creation, as I mentioned in Chapter 2; to say otherwise is to succumb to idolatry and to place some object outside of the created world in which we live.

Scriptures are also clear that just as humanity has "fallen" so have the Powers. Being fallen means that "[e]ach Power exists in a perpetual confusion with respect to its origins, its own identity and its end."[34] Moreover, the various Powers do not function to serve humanity, but instead dominate human life and hinder that life from being lived to the fullest extent possible. "[O]ne of the more unfortunate features of the Powers is their penchant for twisted use of language in order to deceive: denials of truth, doublespeak, 'overtalk,' secrecy, impressions of expertise, surveillance and harassment, exaggeration, deception, cursing, conjuring, diversion and demonization to name a few."[35] The internet, as Power, participates in several of these forms of speech; some of those that relate to the first section of this chapter might be deception, secrecy, and impressions of expertise.

One of the ways in which the Powers and Principalities act against Christ is by portraying themselves as better or different than they are. We humans are too prone to believing that we make

---

[33] John Howard Yoder, *The Politics of Jesus*, Second Edition (Grand Rapids, MI: Eerdmans Publishing Company, 1994), 141.

[34] Brad Kallenberg, *God and Gadgets: Following Jesus in a Technological Age* (Eugene, OR: Cascade Books, 2011), 119.

[35] William Stringfellow, "Traits of the Principalities," in A *Keeper of the Word: Selected Writings of William Stringfellow*, Bill Wylie Kellerman, ed., 204–13 (Grand Rapids, MI: Eerdmans Publishing Company, 1994). Cited in Kallenberg, *God and Gadgets*, 119.

institutions like the internet. But it is exactly in believing this that makes the Powers seem to have autonomy from God; thus they dominate and dehumanize humans by separating us, too, from God. Failure to see that the internet is part of the world of Powers and Principalities allows people not to see various problems associated with internet use. William Stringfellow writes specifically about the way technological culture, as Power, seduces us: "The neglect in moral theology, as that has developed in American ethos, of the demonic powers is startling and virtually inexplicable, when one pauses to think of the exceptional proliferation and sophistication of institutional life, as well as that of other species of the principalities, in *technological culture*."[36] On Stringfellow's view, technological life overtakes us and blinds us to the realities in which we live, leaving us powerless to think about how to be and act in the world.

Part of acknowledging that the internet is affected by the Powers and Principalities is also to acknowledge what the scriptures say: that Christ has subjugated all the Powers and Principalities. Stringfellow suggests that the Powers are "demonic." Such a view makes it seem that we ought to be rejecting technology outright. However, other authors do not take quite that kind of tone, because they see that in the first place, all of creation is God's, and that Christ has redeemed everything, including the Powers. Thus, John Howard Yoder suggests,

[B]asically good creaturely structures can nonetheless be oppressive, and basically selfish decisions can sometimes nonetheless have less evil outcomes. . . The challenge to which the proclamation of Christ's rule over the rebellious world speaks a word of grace is not a problem within the self but a split within the cosmos.[37]

On Yoder's view, we are always participating in a world that both is good and has turned away from being good. The split between good and evil does not ultimately define the world, for Christ has redeemed the world. The Powers, however, still struggle to be emancipated from Christ's authority and so continue to look

---

[36] William Stringfellow, *An Ethic for Christians and Other Aliens in a Strange Land* (Eugene, OR: Wipf and Stock, 2004), 16–7. Emphasis mine.

[37] Yoder, 161.

powerful to us humans, in this in-between time as we wait for Christ's return.

Yoder's "split of the cosmos" aptly describes one of the problems with discussing the internet theologically. Debates about the internet have often come down to being "good" or "bad." This dichotomy leads authors writing about the internet to place themselves on one side or the other, or earnestly trying to name that the internet is both. In her introduction to *Tweet if You [Heart] Jesus*, Elizabeth Drescher writes: "I. . .write from the perspective of a 'digital optimist' – someone who believes that on balance the social benefits of digital technologies outweigh the very real risks. But I would nonetheless characterize myself as a 'digital realist.'"[38] For myself, despite that I see key pieces of theological conversation missing in the internet conversations I witness, I cannot deny that I am fascinated and heartened by seeing lay people grapple with real theological questions, unlike the disinterest of the lay people I often see in the classroom – and their grappling has import and impact. The attempts to place the internet as either good or bad, and desire simply to give up and name it as both, are evidence that the internet itself is a Power, which marks it not only as part of God's good creation, but also as fallen.

What does it mean, then, to describe the Powers as redeemed? From the vantage point of considering the internet, Brad Kallenberg suggests two points. First, naming the internet as redeemed means that Christians might discern how to use the internet "to imagine and enact the reign that began in Christ. . .Our job is, as always, to witness. Even Technology can be turned to this godly purpose."[39] Second, Kallenberg suggests that we might find ways in which the internet actually reveals God in Christ and point that out. Thus, rather than allowing the internet to conceal its power from us, we can turn the internet toward revealing truth.

How do Christians turn the internet toward better purposes? Theologian Marva Dawn has suggested two main ways. First, following John Howard Yoder, she suggests that the internet and other Powers need to be "tamed." This taming can only be done

---

[38] Elizabeth Drescher, *Tweet if You [Heart] Jesus: Practicing Church in the Digital Reformation* Kindle Edition (New York: Morehouse Publishing, 2011), loc. 209.

[39] Kallenberg, 120.

through the "community of those who seek to follow Jesus." That community, the church, is "the primary social structure through which other structures can be changed and that the pattern is one of 'creative transformation' through 'revolutionary subordination.' Thus the Powers will be neither destroyed, nor 'Christianized,' but rather 'tamed'."[40] Markus Barth exemplifies Dawn's point:

> The saints will learn that institutions, if made 'to know' their place, can change. A state can cease from open or secret persecution of the Church. It can change from a tyrannical and chaotic order to a more dignified one that respects the freedom and right of both society and the individual.... As one form of institution follows another, it seldom can be held that each time the newer is better in all respects than the older, or that it will remain any better in the future.... And the newer institutions and orders will change, technology too, when signs of rebellion prove them to be against Christ's throne.[41]

What Barth says is quite pertinent for internet theology. To the extent that the internet represents a new facet of human life, it is clear that this facet is not "better in all respects than the older." Rather, as we live with this new technology, we, as the community of Christ, identify ways in which it is "against Christ's throne." We seek to tame the Powers, not of our own accord, but rather we join in "God's endeavor to bend [the Powers] back to their divine purposes."[42]

Second, Dawn emphasizes the need to live in apparent weakness, for it is by weakness that God defeats the Powers. The prime example is the mystery of Christ having overcome the Powers even through his death. How can Christians make sense of this: through weakness, Powers are defeated? Through weakness, a different kind of power and authority is demonstrated. Debates about the Powers follow along similar lines as the largest debates about the internet: To what extent are the Powers good or bad? Theologians

---

[40] Dawn, Chapter 1.

[41] Dawn, locs 309–15.

[42] Walter Wink, *The Powers that Be: Theology for a New Millennium* (New York: Three Rivers Press, 1999), 35.

thus feel compelled to answer one way or the other. Dawn, however, advocates answering the question about how weakness triumphs over power, instead. This is the more fruitful question, because it helps Christians see where God might be acting, even in so strange a place as the internet.

In fact, what we discover is that the Powers' weakness is that they overblow their own accounts of themselves, which in turn leads to setting up dichotomies that appear to be at war, as in the present debate. In the same passage where Paul discusses that Christ has subjugated the Powers, he also mentions how Jesus does it. He says, "For in him all the fullness of God was pleased to dwell, and through him God was pleased to reconcile to himself all things, whether on earth or in heaven, by making peace through the blood of his cross."[43] Christ is the reconciler and peacemaker among such dichotomous elements-at-war. All things, even the internet, thus demonstrates this reconciling power of Christ's blood, if only we resist naming the internet as wholly bad or good, but instead name it for what it is: part of fallen creation, but capable of redemption.

Thus, I suspect that where God will be on the internet is in the narrow space between overly loving the internet and overly castigating it. On the internet, perhaps it is even in the so-called war itself that we might see Christ's reconciliation. Consider, for example, the groups that Vince Miller is concerned about because they represent "special interest groups" that are overly closed in on themselves. In real-life arenas, these groups have physical means to close out ideas, because they can simply lock their meeting rooms. Online, however, even if a group expels a member from its technological space, a person can still link to the site and raise questions. Carl Elliot's apotemnophiliacs may be an example of the kind of special interest groups Miller discusses; above I raised the point that it was because of the internet that these would-be amputees find a group that validates their self-made identity without also having to raise questions about whether their desires were fulfilling for humans. Here, I suggest that the fact that the internet is both "good" and "bad" means that people can raise questions and link to group sites. Group members can always elect not to see those questions, and may regularly do so. Yet, there is a chance of

---

[43] Colossians 1:19–20, NRSV.

encounter, and a very narrow entry point for discussion with others online that perhaps exists less often offline.

Ultimately, what I am arguing is that Christians need to see how the internet masks its power and then use that knowledge to set the terms of their own theological debates and actions online. Alasdair MacIntyre suggests in his book *Whose Justice? Which Rationality?* that part of Thomas Aquinas' genius is that he set the terms of the debate in which he found himself. MacIntyre writes:

> [w]hat effectively happened was that those rivals came to determine the terms of public fifteenth and sixteenth-century philosophical debate, so that followers of Aquinas were confronted with a dilemma, albeit one which neither they nor their opponents generally recognized. Either, that is to say, they refused to accept the terms of contemporary debate and in so doing isolated themselves and were treated as irrelevant, or they made the mistake of accepting those terms of debate and on those terms seemed to have been defeated. Aquinas' thirteenth-century achievement had been to insist upon setting the terms for debate and enquiry. It was generally, even if not quite always, the misfortune of his fifteenth- and sixteenth-century heirs either not to perceive the need to do so or to fail in attempting to do so.[44]

What MacIntyre suggests of theology in the fifteenth and sixteenth century is true for today. How often do Christians, academic theologians among them, dismiss Web 2.0 spaces, particularly social networking, in favor of the more "serious work" of working in real-life soup kitchens or teaching real-life students? Yet I hope I have demonstrated that such a dichotomy will not work. Theological conversation happens online, and that is where most of God's people are paying attention and getting their own theological questions answered, for good or ill. This is particularly important, especially in a Christian American culture that has been redeveloping anti-intellectual tendencies, and in a culture at large that has seen the resurgence of atheism. Christians have perceived a loss of their authority within nonvirtual cultures, and that gets compounded by the fact that as a group we do not believe we have an authoritative Web 2.0 presence either. We must discover, again, how earthly

---

[44] MacIntyre, 207.

Powers and Principalities operate, and how God's authority acts against them, even and especially online.

To put authority in God's hands and say that the internet has authority only through God requires recognition that God is "on" the internet, or rather that the internet participates in God's life, in the same way that all of God's creation participates in God's life.

Conclusion

I have alluded to one way Christians, online and offline, might respond to the Power of the internet, by setting the terms of the debate. This does not mean arbitrarily closing off certain kinds of sources, as some have sought to do, but instead to name clearly why and how sources pander to the internet's power over us. Rather than limiting sources, Christians might instead have discussions about how to discern better and worse sources of information; they might cultivate a kind of practical wisdom about this. And, instead of allowing scripture to be read in small online "bites," Christians might promote some of reasons for reading scripture slowly, apart from the internet, while at the same time suggest some of the goods that reading scriptures online might involve.

Another way to set the terms of the debate is to place internet theology squarely in its context in both human history and the history of salvation. That is to say, having an understanding of scripture online and offline requires some kind of acknowledgment that there would be no ability to have internet theology without already having these sources received through time, from many different communities. And, as I have endeavored to show in this chapter, having a proper understanding of the internet in relation to God requires understanding not only our place in God's salvation, but also the internet's place as a fallen creature, capable of being redeemed.

What is still an open question, though, is how Christians can set the terms of the debate in ways like these without also falling into the trap of becoming yet another "special interest group." Stanley Hauerwas suggests a possible answer by way of examining the nature of authority: "...the very meaning of authority is community-dependent. Though authority is often confused with power or coercion, it draws its life from community in a quite different manner."[45] Hauerwas suggests that authority is derived because of the needs of a particular community. In this case, authority derives from various Christian communities' needs to witness faithfully to God in an internet age.

Thus, we need to turn more fully to considering Christian communities online. Can the church exist online in such a way that it can help set the terms of the debate? Can Christian "communities" even exist online? And if they do, how can we begin to distinguish communities that will lead toward faithful discipleship and those that simply collaborative with the internet as Power? So, we turn to internet ecclesiology and discussions about the church online.

---

[45] Stanley Hauerwas, *A Community of Character: Toward a Constructive Christian Social Ethic* (Notre Dame, IN: University of Notre Dame Press, 1981), 60.

5

Asking "whether an internet church can exist?" is asking the wrong question

A conversation about the first Internet baptism[1]

Daniel Berman:

> One could get into all sorts of theological debates about reasons, motivations, and intent to the point that [it's] very easy to analyze this situation to death. But the reality is that it was public, it was theologically sound in regards to the specific person involved, and she was immersed (Sorry [it's] the Baptist coming through).[2]

---

[1] FRCInternet, "Flamingo Road Church First Internet Baptism," *YouTube*, (March 22, 2008) http://www.youtube.com/watch?v=qThUe1-RvXU. Accessed February, 2011.

[2] Comment at John Saddington, "World First? Internet Baptism at Flamingo Church", *ChurchMag*, (September 14, 2009) http://churchm.ag/world-first-internet-baptism-by-flamingo-road. Accessed September 16, 2011.

Joannamuses:

> I think it makes a mockery of baptism to turn it into an internet spectacle. I really think this is pushing the online church thing a bit too far. . . . I'm not bothered that a baptism may have needed to happen for some reason without a pastor present in the same location (although certainly good if they are). It also doesn't bother me that such an event may be internet streamed for friends and family who are unable to attend in person. What is bothering me about this is putting this up on youtube [sic] for people with no connection to this wom[a]n to watch.[3]

Introduction

Unlike the other theological doctrines and conversations I reflect on in this book, where offline theological conversations often do not display cognizance of online conversations, conversations about the internet and church occur online *and* offline. In the other chapters, I begin with the internet conversation and the questions it raises on a particular doctrinal concern. When it comes to ecclesiology, however, there are numerous books and articles about the necessity of planting churches online;[4] about the necessity of being the embodied church offline;[5] about the ways that brick-and-mortar churches can learn from online communities (even non-Christian communities),[6] and (rarely) what online communities can learn

---

[3] Comment at John Saddington, "World First? Internet Baptism at Flamingo Church", *ChurchMag*, (September 14, 2009) http://churchm.ag/world-first-internet-baptism-by-flamingo-road. Accessed September 16, 2011.

[4] For example, Douglas Estes, *SimChurch: Being the Church in the Virtual World* (Grand Rapids, MI: Zondervan, 2009).

[5] See Shane Hipps, *Flickering Pixels: How Technology Shapes Your Faith* (Grand Rapids, MI: Zondervan, 2009); Brad Kallenberg, *God and Gadgets: Following Jesus in a Technological Age* (Eugene, OR: Cascade, 2011).

[6] Dwight Friesen, *Thy Kingdom Connected: What the Church Can Learn from Facebook, the Internet, and Other Networks* (Chicago, IL: Baker Books, 2009); Jesse Rice, *The Church of Facebook: How the Hyperconnected are Redefining Community* (Colorado Springs, CO: David C. Cook, 2009).

from brick-and-mortar churches.[7] This conversation demonstrates significant collusion in online and offline theological reflections. My meditations therefore show this collusion.

What I hope to do in this chapter is not only discuss the ways both online and offline theologians speak about "church" and the possibility of Christian community online, but also show that the current conversation does not ask the best kinds of questions to ask if we are to think about the internet as a creature and as a Power. The discussion has been, by and large, on whether internet churches and Christian communities exist, and whether that is good or bad. Assessment of whether internet churches exist and their relative goodness or badness often gets determined in relation to what Christians *do*, as Christians, when they get together, and then whether those things they do should exist online.[8] For example, Christians pray together; read and comment on scripture, saints, and other topics; listen to homilies; meet with each other and discuss issues with their clergy and bishops, and so on, online. Can these activities exist well, when done online? To ask the question in this way avoids perhaps a more important question: Given that Christians are online, what kind of people are we to be? How will we be faithful to Christ, online?

The conversation at the heading of this chapter displays the contrast between the two kinds of questions well: the first correspondent dismisses concerns that an internet baptism, done online, might be a problem by making the case that all the proper elements, especially the visual elements, were present; that the internet was also present is a moot point. Once again, we see the "internet as tool" motif appearing, this time, in aid of baptism into the life, death, and resurrection of Christ. Notice how the first and second correspondents are speaking past each other, though, for the second correspondent's concern is not with the efficacy of this baptism as such, but with the nature of the community gathered to

---

[7] To a certain extent, Elizabeth Drescher discusses this in *Tweet if you [Heart] Jesus: Practicing Church in the Digital Reformation* (New York: Morehouse Publishing, 2011).

[8] So now my readers can see that this is a key reason I wrote this book. "Whether theology exists and whether it is good or bad?" is a similar kind of question to these. My aim has been to suggest that if we believe in the God Jesus Christ reveals, there is no place where we can say theology does not "exist." Rather, the question must be to address the extent to which our theological gazing is faithful to what God has revealed to Christians via church, scripture, sacraments, and so on – or not.

surround the woman being baptized. The second correspondent is concerned about who it is being called upon to witness the online baptism. What does it mean that just anyone, even someone who cares very, very little, if at all, about the meaning of this baptism, could voyeuristically watch the baptism online?

I suggest that an attempt to make an intelligible demarcation between online and offline Christian communities, or even to make an intelligible distinction between community and church, based mostly on what it *does*, fails. An internet ecclesiology needs to focus on a second kind of question, on the kind of community gathered to be Christ's Body. That is to say: "Given that the church exists, what kind of community ought church members be?"[9] Notice that in phrasing the question in this way, I am not making a distinction about the church being "online" or "offline." Indeed, to raise questions about "online" or "offline" *first* enables the internet as a Power to maintain a deceptive hold on us, rather than the other way around, because this kind of dichotomy encourages us either to accept or to reject online and offline spaces on the whole, and thereby either engage the internet in unreflective ways, or reject the possibility of God's working in, on, and through the internet as creature.

So instead, I am making a statement of fact about Jesus Christ: Christ has given the church, his Body, to and for the world. Based on my account thus far about the internet as a creature, I presume that this means the church has, in some way, some kind of relationship with "the internet" as a creature, similar to how the church and its members necessarily interact with other creatures of this world, all the while witnessing to Christ. That relationship is what I am interested in investigating here.

I recognize that saying all this leaves all kinds of good, related questions unasked and unanswered, including important questions about the nature of the church, sacraments, clergy, the physical

---

[9] Of course, I am doing a riff here on my doctoral advisor's many statements suggesting that the question is, "What kind of community ought we be?" In his essay on *Watership Down*, for example, Stanley Hauerwas writes: "we must challenge ourselves to be the kind of community where such a story can be told and manifested by a people formed in accordance with it – for if you believe that Jesus is the messiah of Israel, then 'everything else follows, doesn't it'?" "A Story-Formed Community: Reflections on *Watership Down*" in *The Hauerwas Reader*, eds John Berkman and Michael Cartwright (Durham: Duke University Press, 2001): 171–99, 198.

reality of the church over against an invisible reality, and so on.[10] I recognize, too, that the answers to these other questions have some bearing on a person's answer to "what kind of community ought the church be?" Nonetheless, when it comes to thinking ecclesiologically on the internet, it is the question of the kind of community Christians ought to be that best enables good theological conversation, as I shall try to show.

Accordingly, I will first showcase how conversation about the question of online churches has often proceeded: to see online churches as a new possibility that churches ought to do, or risk becoming defunct and irrelevant. Then I discuss how this view is not quite correct, by turning primarily to internet theologians who reflect on the online communities they encounter. Finally, I will offer some thoughts on what it means to begin with considering the "kind of community" Christians ought to be.

Before I begin this chapter, one additional comment is perhaps necessary. I have often heard people wonder whether "community" is even possible online since it is not clear to them that humans meeting online can relate to each other in significant enough ways to form communities. For the purposes of this chapter, I am presuming that online communities exist, in part because internet users perceive themselves to be part of communities much of the time, though they recognize that community online is not a given. One non-Christian author says: "The internet, like a city, can be an extremely isolating place to exist and take up space, or it can provide a wealth of opportunities to connect with other people and to develop means of self-expression."[11] Researcher Heidi Campbell says she began noticing a change in her human studies participants. They "began to view religious community in terms of their relationship or ideological connection, rather than institutional structures."[12] That is to say, whether due to online or offline influences, people have an understanding that online community exists because it involves relationships. I think it is impossible that humans can encounter

---

[10] Indeed, I am sure that the fact I am Roman Catholic necessarily shapes how I have considered all the theological questions in this book.

[11] Audacia Ray, *Naked on the Internet: Hookups, Downloads, and Chasing in on Internet Exploitation* (Emeryville, CA: Seal Press, 2007), 12.

[12] Heidi Campbell, *Exploring Religious Community Online: We Are One in the Network* (New York: Peter Lang, 2005), 36.

each other, whether in significant or insignificant relationships, and *not* have that relationship affect human communities in some way, for better or for worse.

The internet church as the next new thing. . .

For many theologians, the internet is simply the next phase of existence for the church, the next new frontier and churches need to recognize that their survival depends on changing to conform to this reality. For example, one web observer notes: "A church['s] natural life cycle of 60 or 70 years. . . . It's normal for a church to survive for a certain duration of time. And, if that church doesn't innovate when things are running well and plateauing, then it will naturally decline and close its doors one day. It's just a matter of time."[13] In this understanding of church history, the church online seems merely to be another change in the way church looks and operates.

Such a view is prevalent. Douglas Estes, author of *SimChurch*, proclaims at the outset of his book that when it comes to virtual churches, "[a] change is occurring in the Christian church, the likes of which has not happened for centuries."[14] Estes argues against those who want to claim that it is not church by suggesting that an internet church is a new way of being Christian in the world. To underscore his point, he compares the experience of worshipping virtually with the experience of visiting churches in East Africa. Both involve cultural shocks; both cause Estes to suggest that ". . . our cultural lens influences what we see as the 'right' and 'wrong' practice of church."[15] Yet virtual churches will develop their own senses of what will be good for a church to do: "It seems likely that culture and technology will push the church at large to

---

[13] D. J. Chuang, "Why Churches Must Innovate or Die," *Learnings @ Leadership Network*, http://learnings.leadnet.org/2009/04/why-churches-must-innovate.html (April 27, 2009). Accessed February 23, 2011.

[14] Estes, 17.

[15] Estes, 106.

become even more 'wiki, wiki' (or, 'faster, faster' as it means in the Hawaiian) – meaning the church, especially virtual churches, will be expected to become more collaborative and decentralized."[16] The church is always changing and the presence of social cyborgs means the church must change for that new reality.

The reason there is culture shock, Estes suggests, is due to modern Western views, not so much about the church, but about bodies. Estes traces a link between many peoples' distaste for some kind of virtual, apparently disembodied church, to our sense that our physical world is what is true, or at least, the best way to access what we know about the world. By contrast, Westerners tend to have a dis-ease with what is "spiritual." That seems too ungrounded, too magical.[17] Like it or not, we need to overcome that distaste and recognize the presence of God on the web.

This new iteration means that our bodies respond to worship in different ways than they have, and that the "rules" as we know them will change. Roman Catholic theologian Nathan Mitchell writes,

> [O]ur attitudes towards 'belonging' have been altered. For the first two millennia, the Church has operated on the principle that if people 'bring their bodies to Church', their minds will gradually follow! Thus, the Church has insisted on Sunday Mass attendance as the principal expression of how Catholics belong to the ecclesia. . . . But if people discover that they can belong to 'virtual communities' and 'chat rooms' online – without ever leaving their homes – what then? Is regular ritual participation really necessary?[18]

Mitchell, Estes, and others all suggest that this new technology will therefore necessarily lead to new worship patterns.

There is an array of self-styled churches online, all seeking to reach people in this new medium. Some online churches, like Flamingo Road, are actually "internet campuses" of offline churches; these internet campuses display web cams of online services, as well as

---

[16] Estes, 106.

[17] Estes, 60–1.

[18] Nathan Mitchell, "Ritual and New Media" in *Cyberspace-Cyberethics-Cybertheology*, Erik Borgman, Stephan van Erp and Hille Haker, eds. (London: SCM Press, 2005), 96.

feature online chats for Bible studies and other group activities. Other internet churches, such as one named St. Pixels, are unconnected to offline churches, but rather have their own websites where people can meet to worship, check in to discussion boards, have group studies, and check in with each other.

Still other online churches make use of computer programs that enable them to create spaces online that look and feel like offline churches. Sometimes these are connected to offline churches, and sometimes not. When Douglas Estes and others speak of churches online, they are especially complimentary of this kind of "virtual church" in the "virtual world." "A virtual world is not an augmented form of the real world, it's not typically a fictional world, and it can be but is not necessarily an imaginary world. Most important for our discussion, a virtual world is more likely than not to be a type of real world in synthetic space."[19] One popular program where these churches are developed is at an online program known as Second Life, where internet users can develop avatars, or graphics, of people that they can then move around in Second Life. The avatars can move, talk, swim, fly, and many other things as they navigate the universe of Second Life. Avatars can also work, buy land, and talk, either by typing words into a screen, or through audio if the computer user has a microphone.

Neal Locke, pastor of First Presbyterian Church of Second Life, writes that he believes virtual realities like Second Life, as opposed to social networks like Facebook and Twitter, will quietly overtake everything else and radically change how we do church. Locke writes:

> Projections by researchers in the technology industry indicate that 80% of active Internet users and Fortune 500 companies will be engaged in some sort of virtual reality platform within two years. Analysis of current participation shows that well over 100 million people already are.[20]

For Estes and Locke, the advantages of virtual churches over bloggers' communities or Facebook communities is that this is an

---

[19] Estes, 24.

[20] Neal Locke, "Virtual World Churches and The Reformed Confessions", *Princeton Theological Review* XVII.2 (Fall 2010): 55–66, 55.

interface that allows for people to interact with each other in real time. Facebook and blogs do not promote Christian community because a person can comment on a blog post long after the fact. By contrast, a church in Second Life is a place where avatars can interact and influence each other and interrupt the worship services.[21] What constitutes a "real church" for Estes (besides that it is Biblically based) is that it has some form of directly interactive community available, which means that it involves a community of people who agree to meet with each other at certain stated times for worship. People affect each other in discernible and immediate ways; face-to-face interactions, even if interactions between avatars, are more likely to cause people to become disciples of Jesus than the intermittent interactions people get on Facebook.

Neal Locke makes a similar point in his essay, especially in relation to the sacraments. Virtual avatars in virtual churches, which interact with each other, are far preferable to other forms of online churches. Locke sifts through several confessions in Reformed traditions to discuss "what the sacraments are and what they do."[22] While he notes that the confessions describe sacraments as being visible signs that communicants physically receive and partake, he also emphasizes that the importance of the sacraments, from a Reformed perspective, is their visible nature. That is, "[t]he efficacy of the sacramental elements (not to be confused with the efficacy of the sacrament) consists not in the taste of the bread nor the temperature of the water, but rather in their ability to function as visible signs, calling to the mind of the participant the thing which they signify."[23] Moreover, from a Reformed perspective, the sacraments are meant "to make a visible distinction between [God's] people and those who were without the Covenant. . . ."[24] A church in Second Life therefore can minister to people, represented by their avatars, by administering sacraments that make this distinction between the people of God and other religions. Furthermore, Locke quotes Oxford professor Paul Fiddes, who suggests that "[a]n avatar can receive the bread and wine of the Eucharist within

---

[21] Estes, 75.

[22] Locke, 60.

[23] Locke, 61.

[24] Ibid.

the logic of the virtual world and it will still be a means of grace, since God is present in a virtual world in a way that is suitable for its inhabitants."[25] These avatar-based interactions end up being reasons that Locke privileges the online world of Second Life.

Estes' and Locke's points made sense to me. So, I decided to create an avatar myself and enter Second Life to look around. I visited Locke's church as well as some of the churches that Estes mentions in his book, such as the Anglican Cathedral of Second Life. Then I tried to find some other churches in Second Life besides the ones that are relatively well known offline and online. At Holy Angels Chapel at Second Life, I listened virtually to Thomas Aquinas' "Tantum Ergo" but found that oddly disconcerting since the hymn is about adoring Christ in the Body and Blood of the Eucharist, but there was no Blessed Sacrament before which to fall. I worried that the music, instead, seemed to be about creating ambience, rather than meaning something "real" as Estes seemed to mean it.

After several visits, I found the Basilica of Second Life. It was an awesome piece of digital architecture: it was crafted much like basilicas in Rome, right down to the details of tapestries hanging on the walls. The basilica came complete with candles to light, places to kneel, an old-fashioned confessional, even a monstrance.

I visited several times, rather awed by the details in the floors and walls and the very structure. (There were no times posted for worship, unlike some of the other churches in Second Life.) On my fourth visit, I finally encountered someone, an avatar dressed in nineteenth-century priestly garb. "Do you wish to confess?" he asked? "You hear confessions?" I asked. "Yes," he said. I asked again, just to make sure. "Are there other worship services?" "No."[26] Interesting, I thought. No masses or other worship services, but a time and space to confess sins. What would that mean, I thought to myself, to make a confession online to an avatar who looked like a priest but whose "real" persona I could not know? In particular, I was curious about the fact that for Roman Catholics, to confess sins in the confessional makes it a sacrament, a particular moment of God's grace, and it requires face-to-face contact and physical presence.

---

[25] Paul Fiddes, "Sacraments in a Virutal World?, *Brownblog*, (June 22, 2009) http://brownblog.info/?p=886. Cited in Locke, 62.

[26] Personal correspondence, February 12, 2011.

Estes might insist that both of these are possible in Second Life because avatars are interacting in direct ways. Indeed, was this part of the "new" church that enthralls so many Christians? Would we all be one day confessing online? Would this remedy the Catholic priest shortage, perhaps? In fact, at around this same time, several friends had forwarded me links announcing that there was now a "confession" app for the iPhone. The news stories had made it sound like a person could now confess via an app, but the reality was not quite that exciting.[27] The app was merely a replica of the paper-and-ink guides one can get at the back of any Catholic Church. These guides help people reflect on their sins, as well as give people a sense of what will happen during the sacrament, what the priest will say, what the penitent is expected to say. While one priest did say he hoped this might make confession "more fun," thus far, there is no real possibility for "online confession" in the Catholic sense, much as some might like that eventuality.

I realized that there was still a further question, even if I were not already concerned: Was the priest who he looked to be? Indeed, was the "church" what it proclaimed to be, tapestries and monstrance notwithstanding? I was suspicious: a "church" that only practiced one of the sacraments could not be a church, at least not in Roman Catholic tradition. (Indeed, it couldn't even be a real basilica, which for Catholics means it is the "pope's church" unless the pope had named it as such, and given it a papal umbrella, one of the symbols of the basilica.)

I visited the Basilica of Second Life one more time. I was surprised to find, again, someone there: a young man kneeling before the monstrance. When he saw me, he immediately jumped up and walked over to where I was standing. "I have never met anyone in a church here before," he remarked. "I have only met one person and it was a priest here," I said. "He wanted to hear my confession." "Have to be careful about that," he said. "You never know whether it's really a priest." "True," I said. "Do you want to have sex with me?" asked the guy, as he started giving me "gifts" of lingerie and sex toys.[28]

---

[27] Fr. Edward L. Beck, "Confession App: Catholic Church Sanctions New iPhone App," *ABC News Online*, (February 8, 2011) http://abcnews.go.com/Technology/confession-app-roman-catholic-church-sanctions-iphone-app/story?id=12866499. Accessed February 8, 2011.

[28] Personal correspondence, February 12, 2011.

A rather interesting and abrupt turn of conversation, which made me feel very much like I was toeing some danger waters in relation to adultery (talk about online and offline spaces colliding!) and I got out of there, fast.[29] Thus ended what I had hoped would be an interesting theological conversation about some of the questions I had already been contemplating about sacraments and confession. But of course, that final Second Life conversation immediately led to other reflections: Was the purpose of this "basilica" to be sexually enticing, exactly because one can have "virtual" sex in a place that looks like my grandmother's church?

Later, I discovered that this was not a unique incident in Second Life. Other Second Life institutions that are often identified with Christians in some way are simply fronts for sexual activity, or at least sexual innuendo. When, for example, my colleague Kelly Johnson, who does work on beggars, poverty, and Christian discipleship, asked, "Where are the beggars?" in Second Life, we decided to try to find some. We were unable to encounter any; we had an even more difficult time finding a homeless shelter that was not a front for X-rated music.

I could have left the whole incident and turned to other ecclesiological conversations I have seen online. Instead, I turned to some of the most vocal internet theologians I know – my Facebook friends, some of whom are professionals and some not – and blabbed the whole incident to them.

Here was where the ecclesiological discussions really started in earnest. My non-Catholic, Free Church friends found it amusing but not especially a problem, since I had avoided both the confession and the sex. But even if I hadn't, the confession, like the sex, was virtual. One even suggested that the person had asked for a "confession" because I could thereby tell titillating secrets, which might have then led to some kind of foreplay. Given what happened later, this seems a plausible account. Yet, I found myself considering that even in an offline context, confession is "virtual" in the sense of "unreal" for many of my non-Catholic friends, for it makes no

---

[29] For more on sex, gender, and sex lives, and the ways in which sexual roles continue to be stratified rather than liberatory in Second Life, see Robert Alan Brookey and Kristopher L. Cannon, "Sex Lives in Second Life," *Critical Studies in Media Communication* 26.2 (June 2009): 154–64.

sense to them that Catholics have a sacrament of reconciliation that involves a priest.

My more sacramentally minded friends, on the other hand, immediately proclaimed this experience as horrifying and not because of the sexual proposition. To give a confession online, in a sacramental sense, could not possibly be right. One friend commenting on my experience linked a YouTube video called "Mass We Pray," which does a spoof on Wii entertainment systems, suggesting that just like we emulate playing tennis using the Wii controls, so we can emulate praying, kneeling, and "24 Unique and Exhilarating Ceremonies" using a screen and Wii-like game system at home (with the handheld remotes in the shape of crosses, of course!).[30] At the film's end, there is an option to "buy" the video, at which point one is directed to a website that proclaims you are a heretic, and in turn, advertises the film *Dante's Inferno*.

The friend who had forwarded this link suggested that the Basilica of the Second Life and the Mass We Pray game both alluded to a technological fantasy that we can do everything better by using it, including being part of a church. This is a heresy, proclaimed my friend, because the technology seems to cater to an individualistic sense of participation in church, where individuals can simply "do church" on their own.

Virtual churches do have the advantage of at least meeting at particular stated times unlike on Facebook, where one can post comments for others to read at a later time. If one attends a virtual church via an avatar, one does indeed meet other avatars and have to encounter others. This interactivity is better than the visit I made to the Basilica, where I was more or less on my own. Moreover, my avatar, or those of others, does not have to represent anything real about particular people at any particular point in time. My Second Life avatar could always be perfectly coiffed and dressed to go; I, at seven in the morning, do not look this way. Nor do I actually sound all that great.[31] Proponents of virtual churches like the ones at Second Life suggest that this is actually an advantage, especially for shut ins, or those who find themselves too busy to get dressed

---

[30] PrayerWorksInt, "Mass: We Pray The Video Game," (November 13, 2009) http://www.youtubc.com/watch?v=nRMiRFJzIKA. Accessed September 15, 2011.

[31] Personal correspondence, February 12, 2011.

and head to church. Still, being able to wear pajamas in the comfort of one's own home is not a good reason to decide that church can be done online, if this "new way" of doing church simply enables me to lie about who I am, or causes me simply to be enticed by the "fun" of the church online without its helping me to become a better disciple.

Online Christian traditions

If we probe these encounters with the virtual church further, however, the underlying impetus is not actually the one so often stated, to make sure that the church is keeping up with the next new way to evangelize so that it doesn't become obsolete. Rather, what *seems* new is actually rather "old"; or put another way, traditions shape online life as much as they shape offline life. While online formats may be changing the way Christians "do" church in some senses, it is still elements from the broad tradition of Christianity that enables Christians to make judgments about whether a Christian community is living up to its purposes of worshipping God and forming disciples. Thus, as I argue in this section that there is never a point where an "online church" is not also related to offline churches.

Consider, for example, my experience in the Basilica of Second Life. It is significant that this online space was made to look like a church, in very ornate style. The architect of that online space was clearly trying to replicate what had been done offline and wanted for people to see connections to offline churches. What is more significant, however, is that there were quite a few clues about whether this "church-looking" building was actually a church, from the outset, even before the question about "sex" in a "church" arose. While it looked like a church, there were no signs announcing worship, as I saw at places where Christians did meet regularly. The "priest" was dressed a bit oddly; there was a monstrance but no mass. There was confession but no other sacrament practiced. The space gives the appearance of being part of many centuries of Catholic tradition, but it jars enough against the tradition to be exposed as a troublesome space, if not a lie. Even if it looks like a church, it is not necessarily a church.

By contrast, there were clues at some of the other Second Life church spaces, such as First Presbyterian Church of Second Life. There, even if no one is present to welcome strangers, there is a clear welcome sign and well-marked signs for when to meet for worship. The space looks very similar to many contemporary-style Presbyterian churches. That church also hosts regular introductory sessions to Second Life as a means of hospitality for new avatars. Here, Christians and others might more readily recognize aspects of a Christian tradition of hospitality and regular worship, at the least. And this church is well attended, a marked contrast to the very small numbers at the Basilica of Second Life. The clues about whether Christians might gather in these spaces and might worship God come from reflecting on the degrees to which these spaces, and the avatars in them, participate in something that maps on to Christian traditions or not.

Estes acknowledges that most internet churches begin with tradition (i.e. the Anglican Church worships in a building that to us "looks" like a church) but this should be only a beginning for the possibilities of the online church. "The negative, though, is that if over the long term, virtual churches only replicate real-world forms – and think and visualize in real-world terms – they will never grasp the potential of being the church in the virtual world."[32] So, for example, the ancient Roman catacombs might be an interesting "place" to worship for a focus on "faith" and that outer space might be a place to worship when discussing evangelism.[33] While I think he is right that it would indeed be interesting to encounter these spaces online, especially if a person has never had the chance, nor likely will have the chance to go see the nonvirtual reality spaces of the catacombs or outer space, such changes end up merely seeming like scene changes in a play. Indeed, there are already Christian communities that take advantage of technology to show PowerPoint slides of the catacombs or the universe. What functional difference is there between even an avatar (even a 3D avatar, for it does seem that 3D virtual reality will be the next new thing), encountering a computer-programmer-generated image of the catacombs, other than that it is cooler to feel surrounded by the rocks in a virtual world than to merely see those same rocks in a PowerPoint image?

---

[32] Estes, 108.

[33] Estes, 114.

Even though Second Life churches look new and can make use of interesting technological designs that cannot be done (at least not quickly) offline, people find and recognize virtual churches precisely because they function like offline churches. They meet collectively at some prestated time; they read scriptures; there is a homily, perhaps shown via webcam at the same time that a preacher preaches the sermon offline. In his essay on his Second Life church, Neal Locke places Second Life in conversation with his Reformed tradition, saying that the debate about the "legitimacy of churches online" must "be solidly grounded in our [Reformed] confessions: How do the confessions define church?"[34] Locke goes on to discuss online churches in relation to "proclamation of the Word" and the sacraments rightly administered, as mentioned in the Barmen Confession, the Westminster Larger Catechism and others, and thereby recognizes the importance of the ways Christianity is traditioned.

Theologian Andrew Walls shows similar kinds of connections again and again in his historical look at the ways Christianity has been lived over the past two thousand years. For example, the Jewish Christians in the first century look vastly different to the more courtly, well-educated Greek-speaking courtesans of the fourth century; the Celtic Christians splashing about in cold water are by turn distinctive from an 1840s community sending missionaries to places like Africa. What holds all these together, asks Walls? It is the person of Jesus Christ, alongside the history and scriptures of the church.[35] But the fact of Jesus' presence is significant, for it is Jesus that constantly reminds Christians that they are not quite "in step" with their surroundings. The Christian community gathers to worship Christ, wherever it is, and that community always shows significant cognizance with other Christian communities, if they are worshipping Christ.

Earlier, I quoted a pastor who observed that "if that church doesn't innovate when things are running well and plateauing, then it will naturally decline and close its doors one day." Yet what Walls shows is that Christians' own history indicates it is not "innovate or die," "use this technology or else." It is instead the person of Christ, and the Body of Christ called to be his witnesses. What my encounters

---

[34] Locke, 55.

[35] Andrew Walls, *The Missionary Movement in Christian History: Studies in Transmission of the Faith* (Maryknoll, NY: Orbis Books, 2000), 6.

at the Basilica of Second Life show are that technology is not going to be the salvation of the church. The "next new thing" cannot simply be something grasped for its own sake, without also paying attention to the way the internet, as Power, operates to deceive. That basilica really was quite beautiful but did not claim the purposes of worship.

Travis Pickell, a seminary student concerned about the advent of virtual churches, uses Walls to make a further point about internet churches that while the church might exist anywhere, it should not ever find a place to be fully comfortable. Pickell quotes Walls on this point:

> The 'indigenizing principle' gives voice to the fact that the gospel can 'make itself at home' in any cultural context (including the idiosyncratic cultural context of Second Life). But 'along with the indigenizing principle . . . the Christian inherits the pilgrim principle, which whispers to him that he has no abiding city and warns him that to be faithful to Christ will put him out of step with his society.'[36]

The internet, as Power, will call us to be "in step" with society while attempting to draw us away from its deceptions, but Christ will not always call Christians to use the internet to be "in step."

How do we know Christ, except through the long traditions of Christians handing down the faith, via scripture, preaching, sacraments, acts of mercy, and so on? Indeed, what Christians say is that Christ witnesses to us, by us. We see Christ in each other,[37] in each of our different bodies and visions and views of the world. That is far more a marvel than whatever new vision the internet can give us.[38] Offline churches, with their long history of attention to

---

[36] Travis Pickell, "'Thou Has Given Me a Body': Theological Anthropology and the Virtual Church," *Princeton Theological Review* XVII.2 (Fall 2010): 67–80, 77.

[37] One of the ways we know this is from the tradition of scripture, handed down; see, for example, Matthew 25:31–46.

[38] And even then, we should remember, it is people who are using the internet. Shane Hipps discusses this in his book: "In the end, every technology is traceable to us. They are extensions of ourselves and amplified imitations of our humanness. And if we humans are created in the image of God, then they are also extensions of god – a highly communicative God. A God always seeking to convey an ever expanding and evolving message. A message that finds perfect expression in the person of Jesus, and eventually the body of Christ – the church." Hipps, 184.

Christian practices and ways of handing down the tradition, remain churches. Insofar as Christian communities online can function as "church", it is only in connection with the church offline.

Longing for and belonging to Christian community

Recognizing that community, and its related traditions, are part of the importance of church, internet theologians display many tensions and anxieties about their Christian communities. They especially reflect long and hard on virtual churches and other online versions of church. For example, at a site addressing the question of how to find and attend a virtual church, Econ476 suggests: "cool, good for super busy people, but wonder if the fellowship could be lost." That is, how great it is not to have to get into a car, drive several minutes, and spend an additional hour or so at church, but instead, wearing pajamas and sipping coffee at the breakfast table, log on to an internet worship service and attend. Yet Econ476 worries about whether relationships become lost.

Another user, MommyTeach, offers this quizzical comment: "How funny, Luckily I love my church and I go there to hang out with my sisters and brothers." While the context is not entirely clear, it seems that MommyTeach finds the whole concept of virtual churches "funny" and is a bit dismissive of it, precisely because of how she identifies her community as a nonvirtual family. Family is a common analogy for church communities; she seems very unsure of whether virtual churches can count as that "family."

Likewise, my opening example of the first internet baptism at Flamingo Road Church Internet Campus raises questions about community, and in that context, about communal traditions. Did this baptism stand up to the tradition's view and practice of baptism, given that there are questions about geographical distance and lack of the pastor's physical presence? The first commenter I quoted clearly sees that it did hold up in relation to tradition: it was public, the right words were said, the pastor was present. The second commenter, however, expresses concern that people "with no connection" might watch this baptism. She is bothered, not by the medium, but by the extra-public nature of this baptism. Most baptisms have a public nature in that they are conducted in front of godparents or other congregational witnesses. The difficulty with this one is that it is not public in the sense of making a confession of faith to mostly other Christians; it is making a confession of faith to an entire world, many of whom simply do not care about, or are downright hostile to, the fact that they are (or can be) witnesses to a baptism. What does it mean to be baptized when one's "community" is the whole world, most of whom are not interested in witnessing to Christ?

Richard Beck reflects on the question of church, the internet, and community in another direction. Beck writes on of the top one hundred theological blogs, has a provocative piece called "How Facebook Killed the Church."[39] The blog post sparked a number of discussions on other blogs, and also applause in many circles because Beck's main thesis is that social media like Facebook are the decisive factor in the decline of offline churches, not because people are doing something "new" online but because they are cementing relationships they already have, online. Beck uses data from his research at Abilene Christian University to suggest that peoples' friends on Facebook are *not* new people they've never met; rather social networking sites maintain and enhance existing relationships. For example, his research data that show that freshman at his university who use Facebook to connect with others at the university have higher retention rates than those who do not make connections via social networking.

Beck further discusses recent Pew Forum data that show that Millennials are less connected to churches than older people (1 in 4 Millennials are unaffiliated, compared with 1 in 5 for Generation X, and 1 in 11 for the Boomer generation.) Why are the Millennials leaving? Beck says that it is not because the Millennials have really changed compared with previous generations, nor because churches have changed; what changed was the advent of technology. Cell phone and Facebook use among Millennials now comprise the social connectivity that people might once have found at church.

---

[39] Richard Beck, "How Facebook Killed the Church," *Experimental Theology: The Thoughts, Articles and Essays of Richard Beck*, (March 5, 2010) http:// experimentaltheology.blogspot.com/2010/03/how facebook-killed-church.html. Accessed March 20, 2011.

Generation X didn't have cell phones. Nor did they have Facebook or text messaging. And you can't tell me that Millennials see the church any differently than Generation X saw it . . . based on the sociological evidence Gen X was much more cynical and anti-establishment when compared to the Millennials. . . . So what happened? Why didn't Gen X leave the church while the Millennials are leaving in droves? The difference between Generations X and Y isn't in their views of the church. It's about those cellphones. It's about relationships and connectivity.[40]

The reason connectivity is the difference, on Beck's view, is that past generations made social connections at church that kept them going, even when they found it irritating or hypocritical. The Millennial generation, however, does not need a physical location to build those kinds of relationships. From Beck's point of view, the main point of "church" for most people is "social connection and affiliation."

At the end of his essay, Beck wrote a curious line that had many of his readers up in arms: "May it Rest in Peace." With those words, Beck seemed to be applauding the death of the offline church that Facebook replaces. This caused commenters to retort that socializing is not the point of the church in the first place, and they berate Beck for so strongly seeming to suggest that it is or should be.

But Beck only seems to be advocating the sociability of Facebook. Now comes the subtlety that Beck includes in his article, but that gets missed by most of his commenters, for Beck responds to his commenters saying that his "May it Rest in Peace" line was meant to be a subtle (too subtle) overthrowing of all that he had written. Beck's comment suggests that he wants this Facebook-era church to die out, that of course, socializing is not the point and that the death of this kind of church is no bad thing. Church is not about socializing, and it is time for Christians to retrieve all that the church is, including its sacraments, its history, and its very way of being.

Elizabeth Drescher, whom we have met in other chapters as the author of *Digital Reformation*, wrote a direct response titled "Facebook doesn't kill churches; churches kill churches."[41]

[40] Ibid.

[41] Elizabeth Drescher, "Facebook doesn't kill churches, churches kill churches," *Religious Dispatches*, (March 16, 2011) http://www.religiondispatches.org/archive/atheologies/4390/facebook_doesn%27t_kill_churches%2C_churches_kill_churches/. Accessed March 20, 2011.

Drescher agrees with Beck's view that people are going where their relationships are, but identifies the root problem as not having to do with developments in technology but with the flawed ways in which churches relate to people in the first place. Drescher notes, for example, the website the Vatican posted for John Paul II's beatification activities: several thousand people "liked" the site, but the site did not allow for relationship development between people who come to the site. But this is on par with offline parishes that likewise do not foster offline relationships. In contrast is Nadia Bolz-Weber's church, which practices interconnectivity in real life and online. "It. . . shares a distributed, de-centered practice of ministry that values the contributions of others. It expresses a practice of social and spiritual interactivity that is woefully absent from most of the Facebook pages, Twitter feeds, and other online locales established by religious institutions, including the way-more-numerically-popular John Paul II Facebook page."

Technology is not the key deciding point, for Drescher; she sees that technology merely underscores what has long been a problem: churches that have little experience with socializing in the first place continue to have little experience socializing.

> But until churches and other religious groups, their leaders, and members feel comfortable interacting with one another around real questions of meaning and value—questions having little to do with doctrine and much to do with practices of compassion and justice—their social media participation will do no more to revitalize declining religious institutions than holding weekly Jazzercise classes in the parish hall.[42]

Elizabeth Drescher suggests that the digital church is only upholding what generations of Christians have already discovered, including Augustine: "In the Digital Reformation, the church can only be a center of spiritual life if, as Augustine insisted, its circumference is everywhere."[43] What Beck, Drescher, and their commenters pinpoint

---

[42] Ibid.

[43] Elizabeth Drescher, "Digital Dust-Up: Lenten Practice in the Digital Reformation," *Elizabeth Drescher, PhD,* (March 19, 2011) http://www.elizabethdrescher.net/ ElizabethdrescherNet/Walking_Together_Blog/Entries/2011/3/19_Digital_Dust-Up__Lenten_Practice_in_the_Digital_Reformation.html. Accessed May 16, 2011.

is that it is *not only the internet church that is capable of deceiving itself, but also offline churches*. So, online and offline Christians end up telling each other about what it means to live as a faithful Christian community.

For example, blogger "tamie" writes about what it takes to reach people who are considered the "unchurched." She says people ask her, as someone who is young and knows young people because she has been a university chaplain, what the church ought to be doing. Much of her list has nothing to do with the internet; in fact, even as a blogger, she advocates an anti-internet perspective:

> 1 Be genuine. Do not under any circumstances try to be trendy or hip, if you are not already intrinsically trendy or hip. If you are a 90-year-old woman who enjoys crocheting and listens to Beethoven, by God be proud of it.
> 2 Stop pretending you have a rock band.[44]

Later on, she also writes: "15. Stop worrying about getting young people into the church. Stop worrying about marketing strategies. Take a deep breath. If there is a God, that God isn't going to die even if there are no more Christians at all."[45] Tamie's argument about "church" is clearly dis-inclined toward bringing in technology for technology's sake. The way she envisions church incorporates a ninety-year-old woman doing crochet and it tends also to incorporate what Albert Borgmann (from Chapter 1) would call focal practices. For example, she extends her discussion of bringing good music into church by saying:

> By 'extraordinary music' I mean genuine music. Soulful music. Well-written, well-composed music. Original music. Four-part harmony music. Funky retro organ music. Hymns. Taize chants. Bluegrass. Steel guitar. Humming. Gospel. We are the church; we have a uber-rich history of amazing music.

Tamie's comments about 90-year old women also highlight a point about Christian communities that mitigates some of what Beck suggests above about socializing. Socializing is, actually, an

---

[44] Tamie, "ah, the church," *the Owls and the Angels*, (November 2010) http://owlrainfeathers.blogspot.com/2010/11/ah-church.html. Accessed March 10, 2011.
[45] Ibid.

important part of being Christian, though it cannot be the only facet of Christian life. But one of the strengths of the church through the centuries has been that we gather as individuals called together by Christ. We are not necessarily people who like each other but yet we come together for prayer and discipleship, and we learn despite each other, to socialize with each other and love each other, a little bit better. In fact, here is exactly where offline Christian communities have the edge over online Christian communities. Online communities, as we saw in Chapter 4, tend to be formed around special interest groups of like-minded individuals. This, combined with the fact that internet search engines and other online architecture serve to narrow our ability to engage with people who are "different" from us, means that offline communities have much to offer, and much to witness, in an internet age.

There was much theological conversation generated by Tamie's blog post, much of it relating to questions about socializing and community and how being the church relates to "real life," Commenter Russ remarks "Perhaps Tamie is suggesting things that the church no longer wants to do. Maybe churchgoers and church leaders have really decided that they just want it to be another frustrating extension of everything else that sucks in our society." Later, he writes: "I admire those of you that do go to church – you're the ones who'll resurrect it. As for this young person, though, I don't go to church because when I go, the church part gets in the way of being with the very people I've gone to see. . . . I'll be at the farmer's market until church gets worthwhile." Here is one "young person" not interested in online church or any church because it is "an extension of everything that sucks in our society." Even internet communities cannot offer anything new or different to Christians, and the church simply replicates what he sees as a problem.

What kind of community ought we to be?

Elizabeth Drescher's point, that the church has a circumference everywhere, makes clear that Christian communities cannot be circumscribed by naming them as "online" or "offline"; furthermore, it would be impossible to do so, since Christians flexibly move between their online and offline communities. Humans collaborate in all kinds of communities; Christians must ask themselves what it takes to be the kind of community that is faithful to Christ. Christian communities cannot be composed only of the hip, cool people who use the internet; Jesus is also pretty clear that his followers include those who are poor. Offline, Christians *should* therefore ask, as my colleague Kelly did, "Where are the beggars?" Online, Christians should ask, as Tamie did, "Where are the ninety year old crocheters?" Moreover, such connections between online and offline communities already exist. Two researchers observe that when they looked at peoples' online and offline activities, "the longer people used the network, the more likely they were to use the Internet for social capital building activities that lead to increased community attachment and involvement,"[46] that is, offline community attachment.

Recognizing this requires that online Christian communities be engaged with offline churches; indeed, I still think it is the case that offline, physical churches still carry and represent Christian witness in particular ways. Online churches do represent something new, in some ways, but something that must be judged in light of the whole of Christian witness. Any online community bears the necessity of showing how it is continuous with the past, precisely because Christians online are forging some new ways of doing witness even as they wrestle with doing so faithfully.

I think that the relationship that exists between online and offline communities means that Christians must evaluate the "kind of community to be" in relation to what Christian communities have been doing, if faithful and fruitful, for two thousand years. That community will be the one that tells, and lives, the story of Christ. But it will also be a community that recognizes what our forays into online technology display: that we are always at risk of mis-stepping, and therefore always in need of forgiveness and grace. What better, then, but to have the people of God online *and* offline, helping each other stumble toward God?

I want to conclude this chapter with what I think is an extraordinary, ongoing, story of how a rather large offline community – the

---

[46] Andrea L. Kavanaugh and Scott J. Patterson, "The Impact of Community Computer Networks on Social Capital and Community Involvement in Blacksburg," in *The Internet in Everyday Life*, Barry Wellman and Caroline A. Haythornthwaite, eds., (Oxford: Blackwell, 2002): 325–44, 339.

Presbyterian Church of America, to be precise – has maybe begun to recover some of its soul, online. I mentioned the problem of racism in relation to being social cyborgs in Chapter 3, where I suggested that we cyborgs were often guilty of being unable even to find people different than ourselves because of the way search engines end up shaping peoples' decisions by limiting the search displays we see. This in turn means that social cyborgs often collude in racist habits (and classist habits and so on) without necessarily intending to do so. Racism need not be a necessary result of online interaction, however, and in this particular instance, it is the theological discussion in and among communities, online and offline, that enables people to own up to some of racist history and habits.

This story begins with Peter Slade, a friend of mine who wrote a book called *Open Friendship in a Closed Society: Mission Mississippi and a Theology of Friendship.*[47] It is a good book that discusses a Christian community in Mississippi that seeks racial reconciliation. As part of the book, Slade discusses the racial history of the Presbyterian Church of America, and intimates that racism provides the basis for the founding of that church. Slade notes: "My book came out without even a whimper of PR from [Oxford University Press] back in the fall of 2009. It had received NO reviews when Anthony Bradley blogged about it on July 2, 2010."[48] Bradley is Reformed, by theological persuasion, and an African-American who typically bashes Black Theology and who would be counted as "conservative" in the American political spectrum. He has appeared as a guest with Glenn Beck, for example.

Bradley may bash Black Theology, but that does not mean he is unconcerned about racism. His review of Slade's book generated a lot of response, especially from people who were astounded to discover the ways that racism existed in the Presbyterian Church of America (PCA). They formed a community online to discuss and reflect on the fact of racial sin.

Other bloggers linked to Bradley's blog, including some of the bigger names in the denomination. As response to both Slade's book and Bradley's blog post mounted, the Chancellor of Reformed

---

[47] *Open Friendship in a Closed Society: Mission Mississippi and a Theology of Friendship* (New York: Oxford University Press, 2009).

[48] Personal correspondence, February 14, 2011. The blog Slade mentions is: http://bradley.chattablogs.com/archives/2010/07/why-didnt-they.html

Theological Seminary (the seminary also figures in Slade's history) wrote a pastoral letter in response. In his letter, the chancellor emphasizes the faith of the people who founded the church and the seminary, and suggests again and again the need to focus on faith rather than on sins:

> [W]e learn from 1 Chronicles 29.28, and indeed the whole counsel of the Word of God, that we do not dig up the sins of our fathers for viewing, but we remember their struggles with brief acknowledgement and focus largely on their faith. The founders of the PCA and RTS were men of God who loved Jesus Christ and wanted to train up faithful Gospel pastors and missionaries who would fulfill God's purposes in the world by founding churches, missions and other seminaries that would carry out the Great Commission of Jesus Christ.[49]

That the president felt the need to respond attests to the power of internet theology for offline communities, even as he seems to sidestep some of the racial issues. Other senior members of the denomination also tacitly recognize the power of internet theology in their responses to Bradley's blog. Ligon Duncan, senior pastor at First Presbyterian Church in Jackson, Mississippi, writes to Bradley about how things are better in Jackson than Slade suggests, but says further: "I'll write more to you privately about this, and perhaps post some facts that Mr. Slade has failed to mention in his book."

At the same time that the chancellor was crafting his responses, though, Covenant College, the undergrad college sponsored by the Presbyterian Church of America, invited Slade to give three lectures in February 2011.[50] The organizers of the lecture series write:

> "We hope he will challenge us to consider how our theology is worked out in our lives, and to be honest about the past and its implications for the present and future in the PCA. We're delighted that he will be with us for this series."

---

[49] http://mikemilton.org/2010/07/09/acknowledge-the-sin-accentuate-the-grace-honor-the-fathers-why-i-love-the-pca-and-rts/

[50] "Dr. Peter Slade to Present Lecture Series," *Covenant College: In All Things Christ Preeminent*, (January 26, 2011) http://www.covenant.edu/news/01.26.11_2. Accessed September 23, 2011.

The lectures were then posted as podcasts for further dissemination for the denomination.[51]

Slade writes that "a number of the key people in the PCA asking questions about race and theology have 'friended' me on facebook – where I posted links to my lectures at Covenant College."[52] He has since been invited to Covenant Seminary to spend time with their Doctor of Ministry students working in urban ministry. Slade says, "The reason given by the organizer. . .is that I have started a conversation in the denomination over its doctrine of the spirituality of the church."[53] Moreover, the PCA community gathered online has been able to have conversations about racism in ways that the offline denomination has not.

This is an ongoing story of an entire denomination struggling to respond to its racist history and be faithful to the gospel. It is a story that involves several kinds of online media (blogging, Facebook, podcasts) as well offline media (books and conferences). In all of this, people work together not only to tell a true story about a racist past, but they also hopefully tell a story about a better future of witnessing to Christ and his grace.

---

[51] For example, Peter Slade, "Another Weird Idea," (February 1, 2011) is found here: http://www.covenant.edu/node/3785.

[52] Personal correspondence, February 14, 2011.

[53] Ibid.

6

Theology of the mean: The internet and the good life?

Promotion video for *Love Wins* by Rob Bell:

> "'Reality check: [Gandhi's] in hell.' Gandhi's in hell? He is? And someone knows this for sure? And felt the need to let the rest of us know?"[1]

YouTube rebuttal video "Jesus Wins":

> "'Reality check: God has forgiven Hitler?' God has forgiven Hitler? He did? And someone knows this for sure? And felt the need to let the rest of us know?"[2]

The internet conversation: Winning or faithfulness?

The theological "conversation" depicted above is an example of dueling web-based videos; one is featured at Rob Bell's website as a

---

[1] "Love Wins," *The Work of Rob Bell* website, (no date), video online, https://www.robbell.com/lovewins. Accessed July 14, 2011.

[2] Bball1989, "Rob Bell – Love Wins (Remake: Jesus Wins)," *YouTube*, (April 19, 2011) http://www.youtube.com/watch?v=pDLCN8GwBHE. Accessed July 14, 2011.

promotion for his book *Love Wins*: The story of Gandhi as a peaceful, thoughtful Hindu merges with Bell's questions about heaven and hell and who is there. The promotional video is tantalizing for its suggestion that Bell supports the idea of universal salvation. The other video quoted is a satirical opposing argument, and looks exactly the same as Bell's video except that the main actor is not Bell. He imitates Bell's mannerisms and style of speaking – but with exactly the opposite charge. Love does not win, Jesus wins. The story of Hitler leads to a realization that everyone is a sinner and no one knows about salvation except if they accept Jesus as Lord and Savior.

Such conversations and parodies happen online every day with Christians who have opposing views on a variety of topics, but Rob Bell is no ordinary Christian. He's a pastor of a mega-church and a best-selling author who caters to evangelical Christians. It is partly Bell's fame that propelled this conversation, causing cheers and jeers. Some evangelical Christians found his video dispiriting and un-Christian; the idea of universal salvation was anathema. Others rallied around the ideas they thought Bell espoused. The conversation online was rampant; bloggers, Tweeters, discussion forum conversations, and obviously, YouTube posters, contributed many and varied comments alternately lambasting or loving Bell. The debate rose to such a pitch that even secular media like the *New York Times* took notice.[3]

The Bell theological controversy highlights yet another important question about online theological conversation. This is not the question Bell raises, on whether and how we are saved, but instead the question is about the very nature of the online conversation itself. Do Christians become meaner because they participate online? As we saw in Chapter 1, one of the frequent charges made against the internet is that it promotes individualism because it is merely one person, one computer. A person need never engage with "real people" but could spend all their time online with "friends" with whom they will never "really" touch or engage fully. Combined with peoples' online mobility, and the ability to enter and leave communities at will, it would seem that people who spend time online merely promote their own selfish desires and wants and

[3] Eric Eckholm, "Pastor Stirs Wrath with his Views on Old Questions," *New York Times*, (March 4, 2011) http://www.nytimes.com/2011/03/05/us/05bell.html. Accessed August 22, 2011.

never participate in uncomfortable conversations nor face how their words or actions affect the person on the "other side" of the screen who lives thousands of miles away. Is this what happens with Bell? Vitriolic language and parody, combined with anonymity, only made Christians do things they wouldn't ordinarily do? Is this "theology of the mean"?

If this is true, the damning factor for Christians is that the charge of individualism raises questions about peoples' ability to be "ethical." In nonacademic, popular terms, ethics usually regards those moments of big crisis and big questions, the times when a "decision" must be made about whistle-blowing or sex or abortion. However, academic theologians tend to see ethics as much more encompassing of human life than this, regarding that all of life is directed toward whether and how Christians ought to follow the dual commandments to love God and neighbor. It is this second view of ethics that I have in mind here. I suggested in Chapter 3 that we are social cyborgs; how, then, do social cyborgs interact with each other? Christian life together is meant to be about "loving neighbor" in the service of loving God; does the internet enable people to do this, and in what ways might it do so?

So, this chapter uses the Bell controversy to examine the charge of individualism and shows that Christians (and others) are, perhaps despite themselves, often being formed by internet communities in ways that are not Christ-like, but this is not necessarily the way online life must work. I will show, too, how some internet communities are doing the opposite: forming and shaping their participants' lives particularly so that they conform to Christ's will. They are practicing virtue ethics, which is another kind of theology of the "mean," because living the virtues means taking a mean, or middle path, between harmful extremes. Indeed, in some cases, Christians online are bringing back some practices that had been left behind. Charges of individualism might still be made, but not about the internet or internet users as a group.

Love Wins?

Rob Bell's book *Love Wins* advances questions about salvation and about who is God. Bell is not the first person to ask these kinds of questions, but he is one of the few to be so thoroughly admonished for his views online. What is particularly interesting is that much of the online conversation occurred well before the book was even released; people were responding to the video about the book. Justin Taylor wrote one of the initial blog responses to the video: "It is unspeakably sad when those called to be ministers of the Word distort the gospel and deceive the people of God with false doctrine."[4] Commenters at the blog quickly took the conversation to heights of venom with INTERNET YELLING and name calling. Just one example suffices: "any Tom, Dick or Harry can say whatsoever they choose to say about God and truth regardless how blatantly they are against the revealed truth of the Scriptures and we have to wait for cloth to confirm it? . . . Why would Peter even bother to warn ALL CHRISTIANS against false prophets? It takes a Universalists to accept one."[5]

Another pastor, John Piper led a Twitter debate by tweeting, "Farewell, Rob Bell" with a link to Taylor's blog post as a way of saying, Bell is no longer one of us. The blogosphere, Twitter, and Facebook were all full of people yelling at each other about Bell's presumed argument. The debate continued for days and weeks – a long time in web time, leading some to suggest that "[t]he Christian community's current *Bellapalooza* is the first evangelical doctrinal debate in history to occur nearly exclusively on the Internet."[6]

The relative noise the conversation generated combined with its length and breadth led a few Christian commentators to reflect on the tone of the conversation itself. Some remarked that this theological conversation displayed some very un-Christianlike character, and all on very, very public display. After over a month of debate, blogger Gary David Stratton reflected: "Meanness Wins!" The blogger continued by quoting Dallas Willard: "Why are Christians so mean?

[4] Justin Taylor, "Rob Bell, Universalist?" *The Gospel Coalition*, (February 26, 2011) http://thegospelcoalition.org/blogs/justintaylor/2011/02/26/rob-bell-universalist. Accessed August 12, 2011.

[5] Ricky, comment, "Rob Bell, Universalist?" *The Gospel Coalition*, (February 26, 2011) http://thegospelcoalition.org/blogs/justintaylor/2011/02/26/rob-bell-universalist. Accessed August 12, 2011. [sic]

[6] Gary David Stratton, "Danger! Angry Blogger: The Apostle Paul's Cyber-relationship Checklist," Two Handed Warriors: Reimagining Faith and Culture One Story at a Time (2011) http://www.garydavidstratton.com/2011/faith-2/cyberspace-wins-an-update-on-the-rob-bell-controversy. Accessed August 22, 2011.

Well, there actually is an answer to that question. . . . Christians are routinely taught by example and word that it is more important to be right. . . than to be Christlike."[7] If Willard is correct, this drive to be "right" takes on a very strange tenor as soon as one realizes how much internet discourse can allow for people to skimp on traditional ways of being fair and making sure one has "got it right." For example, when an offline friend cornered me at a party last week to ask whether she ought to read Rob Bell's book, several other friends joined in. I quickly realized from the conversation that most others at the gathering had already heard of Rob Bell via Twitter or Facebook and so they referred to things they had seen or heard online – yet no one actually had a copy of Bell's book in their possession. Each person had a strong opinion about Bell's "position" but no one was able to state Bell's position as stated in the book because they were basing their information on the video quoted at the beginning of this chapter, or worse, on others' commentary on that video (without having seen the video themselves).

Related to this is that we social cyborgs do have a problem with reading carefully, or with reading at all. This does make us meaner, especially in the sense of being hospitable and generous toward others. It would appear that we lack even the capacity to treat others as we would wish to be treated. Online comments are full of statements from people saying (again, LOUDLY) that they have been misread or misinterpreted. Lack of reading also goes hand in hand with the point I brought up in Chapter 3 about theological anthropology: we only see what computer programs (and programmers) show us, which means that contrary points of view are not easy to come by in internet discourse. The internet's architecture makes skimming very easy because of the way web pages tend to be designed.[8] So it would seem that the very nature of the internet forms us to think about others in ways that are dehumanizing, even before we reflect on the conversations people can have.

---

[7] Ibid.

[8] Mark Bauerlein, *The Dumbest Generation: How the Digital Age Stupefies Young Americans and Jeopardizes Our Future [Or, Don't Trust Anyone Under 30]* (New York: Jeremy P. Tarcher/Penguin, 2008), 143. Bauerlein also discusses some of the other results of web-based reading; for example, students learn fewer words and therefore have not developed capacities to read and digest difficult and complex concepts.

Perhaps meanness really does win, when it comes to internet conversations. Another commenter in the Rob Bell saga writes:

> Do you think it is wrong for Rob Bell to question traditional views of heaven and hell?
> Answer: *I don't care.*
>
> Do you think it is wrong for traditionalist writers to label Rob Bell a universalist?
> Answer: *I don't care.*
>
> Do you think it is wrong for every Christian with an iPhone to tweet their answers to the above questions from restaurant bathrooms and then go home and blog about it?
> Answer: *Now there's an interesting question.*[9]

For him, the concern was not with the theological conversation itself, but the fact that it was happening on the internet. The instantaneity of web communication combines unhelpfully with an individual's desire to be known or to look good for their internet friends to the point that much commentary simply becomes self-aggrandizing, and well, mean.

Social scientific studies do suggest that we are, at the least, more rude online. One 2004 political science study found that twenty percent of the content on political discussion boards could be considered impolite, saying:

> The anonymity of cyberspace makes it easier for individuals to be rude, although not necessarily uncivil. . . .the absence of face-to-face communication fosters discussion that is more heated. . . .[10]

For the purposes of that study, impoliteness was defined as name-calling, casting aspersions (i.e. naming someone as irrational),

---

[9] John Dyer, "Not Many of You Should Presume to Be Bloggers," *Christianity Today* online, (March 3, 2011) http://www.christianitytoday.com/ct/2011/marchweb-only/bloggers.html. Accessed August 22, 2011.

[10] Zizi Papacharrizzi, "Democracy Online," *New Media and Society* 6.2: 259–83, 274. Available online at http://www.ict-21.ch/com-ict/IMG/pdf/DemocracyOnline.pdf. Papcharrizzi is arguing a different point than mine, however. He attempts to distinguish between impolite speech and uncivil speech, and suggests the possibility that online users are often impolite but not uncivil. For him, this suggests that the internet actually enhance democratic participation.

exaggerating content of others' posts, and using derogatory or vulgar speech.[11] The immediacy of the internet further heightens a kneejerk response to people, ideas, and events, often without good reflection. Being "fair" to another person – even online – takes a back seat to getting one's ideas heard, by which is usually meant that people feel the need to comment on or have a say about everything, if they wish.

John Dyer at the *Christianity Today* blog considers James 3:1("Not many of you should become teachers, my brothers and sisters, for you know that we who teach will be judged with greater strictness.")[12] in comparison with the internet discussions he saw arising from the Rob Bell controversy. He says:

> Facebook and Twitter do not encourage this kind of self-restraint [that we see in the James passage]. . . . There is no time for reflection in prayer, no place for discussion with other flesh and blood image bearers, and no incentive to remain silent. You must declare your position, and you must declare it now.[13]

Dyer's thought is that if we felt we could take time to read, reflect, and only then, write and respond, people might have been more charitable toward Bell in at least reading his work before damning him to hell. In his view, the medium itself generates rash, hasty responses, compared with the careful, measured reflection that good theology seeks, or at the least, the kinds of virtuous interactions Christians seek to promote.

Dyer's solution, then, is to suggest that "not many" people should be bloggers, and that bloggers ought to see themselves in the role of being a teacher. "What few of us realize is that when we press those 'Publish', 'Post', 'Comment', and 'Send' buttons, we are making the shift away from merely 'believing' truth and stepping into the arena of publishing that belief. In doing so we are effectively assuming a position of leadership and teaching that prior to 2004 was not available to us."[14] Indeed, on Dyer's view, the kind of free-for-all

---

[11] Ibid.

[12] NRSV.

[13] Dyer, "Not Many Should Presume to be Bloggers."

[14] Ibid.

of the internet is not good for most Christians precisely because they are not careful enough with the faith they are presuming to be transmitting.

People are guilty of escalating online arguments far beyond where they would usually go, because the visceral reality of the other person is not there. (In the same way, a tech guy at my university tells me that students who attempt to write eighty-page master's theses online have less success than those who write them in the context of face-to-face conversations with their advisors. He thinks it has something to do with the immediacy of bodily contact in the second example.) But there is more to it than that. I wonder if our arguments escalate and become so contentious because the person we imagine in space at some point responds in ways that do not reconcile with what we imagine.

Living "the good life" online

If this were the end of all internet interaction, of course it would be frustrating and, indeed, mysterious as to why anyone would wish to be a part of internet spaces. But this is not entirely the end; instead, some people are trying to help each other be better internet users in a variety of internet settings, with the ultimate goal of being better people, both online and offline. Contrary to John Dyer, who thinks not just everyone should blog, Dyer's commentators seek to show a different way of seeing and interpreting online life. Bernie Persson writes, "It's true that there's a lot of hot air on the internet, and anyone can get their opinion out there, but often it's hardly heard. A few bloggers do rise to the top, but that's either because what they write is well-thought out, well-argued and is wise, or because what they say is populist in some way. . ."[15] Persson's point is that internet conversation need not necessarily be "hot air" and that, in fact, the best conversations are the ones that contain the same kinds of sought-after qualities as off-line work: well thought out, well argued, wise.

---

[15] Bernie Persson, Comment, "Not All Should Presume to be Bloggers," *Christianity Today* online, (March 25, 2011) http://www.christianitytoday.com/ct/2011/marchweb-only/bloggers.html. Accessed July 27, 2011.

In other words, even though in some ways using the internet on iPhones and computers as individuals seems to promote a kind of selfishness and interiority, it is also the case that internet users are discerning about who comprises the best among them. They are people who exhibit certain kinds of qualities; these are the people who tend to be heard online. In ethical terminology, we might name these qualities as "virtues."

Virtue ethics aims to develop peoples' characters; the way we shape and form character is through habitually practicing the qualities we hope to become. Virtues are considered good practices; vices are habits that induce the opposite characteristics that people desire. So, for example, practicing hospitality lends toward a person becoming a more generous, hospitable person; practicing miserliness lends toward a person becoming more suspicious of others. While virtue theory is not unique to Christianity, Christians have long seen the importance of virtue for living a good life. The end toward which Christians aim is life and friendship with God. Therefore, all virtues must be linked to that life and friendship with God.

One important aspect of virtue is that it is a "mean" between two extremes. A person seeking to have certain qualities to their character wants just the right amount, not too much or too little. Courage is commonly seen as a virtue, for example, but too much courage can lead a person to be arrogant, doing things too rashly, concerned more to demonstrate "strength" for show rather than through some desire for real courage. Being macho might be a vice that hurts people more than it helps. On the other extreme, having too little courage – cowardice – means that a person never does a good act because of perceived danger. Cowardice, too, hurts people.

Above, I suggested a "theology of the mean" in terms of meanness, but here I suggest that some internet theologians are actively developing a "theology of the mean" in terms of virtue, in terms of finding the appropriate and best ways to act so that one shows neither too little nor too much of a particular quality and habit. Bernie Persson names some virtues in the comment above: thoughtfulness, wisdom, and arguing well. What does it take to learn these, and how does a person know when they are being thoughtful rather than thoughtless or overbearing? How does one know they are being wise or arguing well? Part of the answer to those questions is that learning to live virtuously requires a community of people who have a shared end in mind so that they know what good habits are necessary for attaining that end. Learning to live well requires that a person have "moral exemplars" or people who are living examples of how to do something well.

Some Christian bloggers might be considered such moral exemplars; these are also the bloggers who have had blog discussions about the ways to live well. These discussions on living well in turn give rise to communal guidelines and rules, which provide a fascinating look into the ways people conduct practical reasoning about good behavior. Thus, in reflecting on the Rob Bell fiasco, Gary David Stratton proposed a "St. Paul's Checklist" for bloggers, in which he asks, for example, whether the post is "kind," "devoid of boasting," or "self-seeking."[16] Each of these terms denotes virtues and vices; each of these terms provides a way for individuals and communities to reflect on the extent to which they are living as Christian witnesses online.

Similarly, Rachel Held Evans and her blog commentators reflected at length, and partly because of the Bell controversy, about what it means to be a Christian online, and not just on the blog. Among the thoughts:

1 Avoid the passive–aggressive Facebook status. (E.g.: "Christie Christianson prays that the Holy Spirit will convict certain people regarding certain over-the-top Vacation Bible School themes.")

2 Remember that breaking fellowship via Twitter is just as bad as breaking up via text.

3 How many Bible verses are included in the comment? If it's more than five, it's not a comment, it's a bibliography. . . .

6 Try to read blog posts, books, and articles in their entirety before writing a comment or review.

7 If you suspect you might have a sin[ful] nature like everyone else on the planet, consider waiting a few minutes before you broadcast your first reaction across the Internet.[17]

---

[16] Stratton, http://www.garydavidstratton.com/2011/faith-2/cyberspace-wins-an-update-on-the-rob-bell-controversy.

[17] Rachel Held Evans, "A Christian's Guide to Not Being A Jerk on the Internet," *Rachel Held Evans Author Speaker Blogger,* (May 4, 2011) http://rachelheldevans.com/christian-guide-internet. Accessed July 18, 2011.

Checklists like these attempt to use Christian sources (such as scripture or doctrine) to shape Christians' views of how to interact online. Of course, they are voluntary; bloggers like Evans who have large readerships hope that their reflections will encourage readers to reflect on their own actions, resulting in less "theology of the mean" and more of the grace, courtesy, and goodwill appropriate to living a Christian life.

Internet users are often aware of the ways in which the people they interact with are coming across in poor ways, and they use this knowledge then to reflect on their own behavior. For example, one commenter at Evans' blog discusses "internet courage," noting that the true virtue needs to be something that is said not only online but that a person would be willing to say face to face, as well. "Is this post internet courage? I.e., would you be willing to say this to the person's face, or are you only brave enough to say this here because you feel non-threatened doing it over the internet? This falls both under acting out of fear rather than love, and manipulation."[18] True courage, whether in an internet posting or in an offline conversation, will still exhibit the same kinds of habits. In some studies, online members have also identified certain virtues as being especially valued in online communities, for example, "relationship, care, value, connection, and intimate communication" as well as shared faith.[19]

Bloggers like Evans and Stratton would agree with John Dyer that people are often not being Christ-like online, and that the Rob Bell controversy especially exhibited bad behaviors. Yet for Evans, Stratton, and others, the solution is not to disengage from the internet but to engage it in better ways. "Not everyone should presume to be bloggers" becomes "Christians need to blog well." Checklists, communal guidelines, and rules provide ways for Christians online to help each other think through their actions so that they can become more the people they wish to be.

Part of what we can see at work in these communal guidelines and checklists is the development of what ethicists call "practical

---

[18] Todd Erickson, Comment, "A Christian's Guide to Not Being a Jerk on the Internet," *Rachel Held Evans Author Speaker Blogger,* (no date) http://rachelheldevans.com/christian-guide-internet. Accessed July 18, 2011.

[19] Heidi Campbell, *Exploring Religious Community Online* (New York: Peter Lang, 2005), 181.

wisdom" or "practical reasoning." Unlike theoretical reasoning, practical reasoning involves learning while doing. The example I often give my students is the difference between using a recipe card to bake bread and using my mother (a stellar baker) to bake bread. The recipe card presents theoretical knowledge; it abstractly records approximations of the amount of flour, yeast, water, sugar, oil, and other ingredients needed to bake bread, and the approximate time and temperature needed to bake bread. The recipe card can describe, to some extent, the actions needed to bake bread, such as kneading. But to someone who has never ever seen another person bake bread will still have some difficulty figuring out what "kneading" is, or how long to do it, or how hard to knead. Someone relying on the theoretical knowledge of the recipe card to bake bread and who has never baked bread before might well bake a good loaf of bread, but the fact that they did is rather a matter of luck. Recipe cards really do only present approximations of knowledge; the amount of flour one "really" needs is dependent on all kinds of things the recipe card cannot name: how large the measuring cups are, how accurate the scale and the oven thermometer are, how humid the day is, how cold the baking area is, and so on. Accordingly, the new-fledged baker is just as likely to have baked a loaf that is too dense, too tough, doesn't rise, cracks in the middle, has a grainy texture, and all of the other things that can go wrong when baking bread.

If a new baker can watch and learn from my mother's baking, however, that person would have the benefit of fifty years of experience baking bread. Working alongside my mother, the new baker learns, through practice, when yeast is too old, when there is too much flour, when the kitchen is not hot enough, and all the many other nuances that could not possibly fit onto a recipe card, try as we might. This is practical reasoning, and it requires moral exemplars – people who know how to practice the activity well – alongside a vision of the end goal (i.e. a really good loaf of bread).

The same is true of internet users. They need moral exemplars who show the best ways to do an activity. In online conversation, at least, those online exemplars seem to be emerging as bloggers like Evans, who have large followings, and whose blog is "liked" on Facebook precisely because she raises good, thoughtful questions all while maintaining Christian stance that her audiences can identify.

One of the benefits of developing theological conversation about what is sinful and making use of virtue and practical wisdom, instead of seeing technology use as a dichotomy between online and offline life is that it has the effect of bridging perceived generation gaps between younger people who use technology and adults who don't.[20] This is because practical wisdom allows for reflection even through the changes life takes, while dichotomizing technology and nontechnology, or online and offline space, prevents the ability to think about what it means to act well.

For example, I was recently speaking with a friend about a pamphlet written by the US Conference of Catholic Bishops in the year 2000, which aims to help parents figure out how to navigate technology use at home. One of the suggestions in the pamphlet is that the computer be kept in a public room of the house so that parents can monitor their children's internet use.[21] My friend, the mother of three teenagers, had some rather derisory comments, for in these days of instantaneous wireless communication, the idea of being able to confine a computer to one room seems quaint. Yet note: the bishops did not advocate total disengagement with technology, but instead their rules advocate enabling parents to help their kids think through internet use.

Additionally, I wonder if a move away from dichotomizing online and offline life might actually have the affect of remembering that regardless of what we are doing, we are always embodied, because what it means to be human is partly that we do have bodies. Online, this means remembering the humans on the "other end" of the screen and they can be hurt; offline, this means remembering that people are real, not simply screen entities, and again, they can be hurt.

As technologies have developed, others have stepped in to think practically about how to parent children who use these technologies. For example, Susan Maushart provides updated suggestions, including "Thou shalt keep thy bedroom a media-free zone," and

---

[20] It is not at all clear that such a gap exists, at least between youth and their parents. For example, in 2010, the percentage of Facebook users ages 18 to 34 is not statistically different from the percentage of Facebook users ages 25 to 54. "The Average Age of Facebook Users Rise," *After Marketer's Club*, (March 13, 2011) http://aftermarketerclub.com/blog/2011/03/the-average-age-of-facebook-users-rise. Accessed August 26, 2011.

[21] "Your Family and Cyberspace: A Statement of the US Catholic Bishops," (Washington, DC: United States Catholic Conference, 2000).

"Thou shalt not text and drive (or talk, or sleep)" that stem from her experiences in turning-off technology for six months.[22] Another important one is "Thou shalt not WILF"[23] (derived from the internet slang for "What Was I Looking For?"), which refers to not wasting time simply surfing the web to find ways to occupy one's time. All of these rules are developed in relation to wanting not to be selfish, but to be engaged well, both online and offline. Practical wisdom, combined with a sense of the end goal Christians seek to attain, allows for rules about internet use to be flexible and yet not to allow merely anything to be acceptable.

To have the "good life" online, you need to be good offline—and vice versa

We have already seen, above, some inkling of how offline and online interactions interrelate. Inherent in the idea of the checklists and commentaries discussed above is that, contrary to the concerns some had about the Rob Bell controversy and what it means for Christians, online life is not so very different from offline life. For example, one commenter on Evans' checklist suggests: "Practice not being a jerk in real life, and your online behavior will follow suit."[24] One might wonder if the reverse is true: practice not being a jerk online and your offline behavior will follow suit. Internet theologians often recognize that what they do online affects and is affected by offline life, for there is no neat, sharp distinction that makes navigating these easy.

Yet for Christians, who must be concerned with loving all their neighbors, whether online or offline, evaluating *both* online and offline moral formations is imperative. It seems to be the case that

---

[22] Susan Maushart, *The Winter of Our Disconnect: How Three Totally Wired Teenagers (and a Mother Who Slept with Her iPhone) Pulled the Plug on their Technology and Lived to Tell the Tale* (New York: Jeremy P. Tarcher/Penguin, 2010), Afterword.

[23] Ibid.

[24] Justin B. Comment, "A Christian's Guide to Not Being A Jerk on the Internet," *Rachel Held Evans Author Speaker Blogger,* (no date) http://rachelheldevans.com/christian-guide-internet. Accessed July 18, 2011.

good online users have been formed well in both online and offline communities; I would go so far as to say that offline Christian community is requirement for good online participation. Note, for example, that Gary David Stratton alludes to scripture in his set of guidelines; Rachel Held Evans explicitly discusses the Christian doctrine of sin in her discussion. Both bloggers presume that their audiences will know and understand what both of these are. How will those online know what these are, or even understand that references to scripture are what Christians "do" unless they have communities that help form them and shape them to recognize the importance of the Bible or doctrine?

Brad Kallenberg discusses the necessity of offline witness in his book *God and Gadgets,* when he talks about the fact that being good Christian witnesses takes time and embodiment. That is partly because being Christian involves learning a new "conceptual" language – a language that has a particular understanding of God (as Triune), that involves singing hymns on Sunday morning, that involves the strange stories encountered in scripture, and so on. This is similar to what I mentioned in Chapter 1; that new languages we learn (such as the medical speech doctors learn, or the engineering speech that engineers learn) entail new ways of thinking and new behaviors. People begin to learn these languages via other people, and Kallenberg suggests that a well-trained engineer has not only learned a new language with words like "truss" and "footing" but also approaches the world in a new way, in behavior and reflection. The same is true of Christians: one can learn to be Christian by being trained by other Christians, especially other Christians who are themselves exemplars of what it means to follow Christ.[25]

The good life online. . .

While I think Kallenberg is right that there is a necessity of offline witness, I also argue that there are some actions and ethical considerations that may fare better in online contexts than in offline contexts. For example, I wonder if, in some cases, internet users are actually being better moral exemplars for certain Christian practices

---

[25] Brad Kallenberg, *God and Gadgets: Following Jesus in a Technological Age* (Eugene, OR: Cascade Books, 2011), see especially Chapter 3.

than offline Christians are. Internet collaboration is so interesting because people online seek out ways to help each other, and for free, in sharp contrast to the ways offline communities eke money from all sorts of situations. (I am thinking, for example, of all the home-grown dent-removal businesses that sprung up overnight following a hail storm; each proprietor promised to be able to remove dents from cars, or replace windows or other structures damaged by hail.) Online communities often operate more in a gift mode than in a capitalist mode in the sense that people enjoy giving each other tips for games, parenting, saving money, taking photographs, and so on, without thought to cost. One of the best examples of this kind of gift community is open source technology developers. Mozilla Firefox, Linux, Zotero, and a whole host of other open-source software are freely available programs that people can also change. Open source communities aim to help people improve programs, and developers revel in being able to make a great idea work.[26]

Related to this is the idea of the "hacker ethic." Hackers tend to be associated with spreading computer viruses or accessing confidential information, but the hacker ethic, as developed by proponent Pekka Himanen, is actually a view of life as a joyful commitment to the pursuit of excellence. Himanen claims that early computer hackers were not interested by money or fame, but by the pursuit of knowledge and the game. In this, it is an anti-utilitarian ethic. The hacker ethic is not limited to computer programming; hacker ethics can infuse teaching, mechanical work, and other jobs and hobbies.[27] In a capitalist world, the internet can actually be the source of resistance against consumerism, utilitarianism, and desires run amok.

Perhaps the real test point of the effect of online interactions is in online video games, however. I have often had images of (and know of) people, often teenage boys, spending lots of time alone in their rooms playing blood-and-gore video games that seem only to make players more closed in on themselves. This vision need not necessarily be the case. Jane McGonigal, author of *Reality is Broken: Why Games Make Us Better and How They Can Change the World,*

---

[26] "Open Source Technology", University of Dayton Technology Conference (2009). Unpublished conference presentation.

[27] Pekka Himanen, *The Hacker Ethic and the Spirit of the Information Age* (New York: Random House, 2001).

points out that many people are gamers (after all, a person playing solitaire is a gamer), and that gamers do perceive effects of their gaming on their online and offline lives. One player of the game *Halo* writes, for example: "*Halo* has always been a place where I feel good. I don't mean that in a James Brown sense. I mean it's a place where I feel virtuous. . . . [It] engenders a sense of honour and duty which actually make you feel like a better person. . . ."[28] Of course, if we only felt better "online" while playing a fantasy game, that would be far less desired than finding ways to become better for real.

One of McGonigal's missions is to develop games that affect "real life" for the better. Why not put this massive amount of time spent online, playing games, to use for good? McGonigal suggests this point in her book about online gaming: that people are discovering, via games, that doing something collectively for a purpose is far more satisfying than doing something individually, focused on ourselves.[29]

One example is with a new venture called "alternate reality games," which are games that people design in order to help themselves, their friends, family, and strangers they have met online learn to be better and make their world better. Alternate reality games are played offline, but are often linked to online contexts. Jane McGonigal, gives several examples, including one about a game she created called "Bounce," which was designed to connect senior citizens with younger generations over the phone. Because seniors often do not have access to the internet, McGonigal designed the game so that only one person needed to have access to the web. The player with web access could log in and find a series of questions ("What's a body of water you've both swum in?")[30] that is meant to prompt discussion until both people find a common connection in answer to the question. Ultimately, the game itself was meant

---

[28] Margaret Robertson, "One More Go: Why *Halo* Makes Me Want to Lay Down and Die," *Offworld*, (September 25, 2009) http://www.offworld.com/2009/09/one-more-go-why-halo-makes-me.html. Cited in Jane McGonigal, *Reality is Broken: Why Games Make Us Better and How They Can Change the World* (New York: The Penguin Press, 2011), 108.

[29] Jane McGonigal, *Reality is Broken*, 111–14.

[30] Jane McGonigal, *Reality is Broken: Why Games Make Us Better and How They Can Change the World* (New York: The Penguin Press, 2011), 179.

to decrease loneliness and isolation members of assisted living and nursing home facilities often feel. From McGonigal's point of view, this was achieved qualitatively.

For McGonigal, the collective of game players is necessary if we want to make a difference, and moreover, we can make a difference via games. An example she gives is another game she developed for the World Bank Institute called "EVOKE." EVOKE is a ten-week game that encourages African players (playing on their mobile phones, since those are readily available sources of technology in Africa) to solve a new mission and quest each week. For example, in the first week, one of the EVOKE missions is to "increase the food security of at least one person in your community."[31] McGonigal reminds players that food security isn't about providing one meal, but rather about finding more permanent solutions to ending hunger. Suggestions for players include building gardens, or making it easier to share food in their own communities. In order to receive points for the missions, the players make a blog post or online video that documents what they did and discovered. Players therefore not only learn ways to help with real-life problems, but can also earn scholarships and mentorships. The first version of the game had 19,000 players from 150 countries.[32] Online communities can provide an escape – a rather meaningful escape from a late-modern consumer reality that does not enable people, on the whole, to be generous, hospitable, kind, or any other host of virtues that can be practiced in online communities.

One of the important points here is that a community – in this case, a non-Christian gaming community – can indeed have rules and practices that form people to live well and also to influence and shape their world for good. Games are especially helpful examples of thinking about ethical behavior, because they have rules and examples of players that excel, whom everyone wants to emulate.

Online theology has an advantage over offline theology, too, in relation to commonly held ethical assumptions. In offline conversation, a prominent assumption is that rules are often arbitrary and carry very little relationship with what is real and

---

[31] McGonigal, 336.

[32] For more examples of what McGonigal sees as large-scale collaborative games, see Chapter 14 of *Reality is Broken*.

true. For example, the current Christian debate about gay marriage often centers on the "rules" churches make about marriage, and how those are particularly unjust in relation to the love that gay couples exhibit toward each other. Suspicion about rules is not limited to gay marriage, of course: almost any hot-button topic is subject to this view of law as arbitrary, unfair, and unhelpful for human life. Laws against euthanasia get cast as being not truly loving of people who are in pain and at the end of their life; laws surrounding abortion get cast as being either unloving of the woman who is now faced with an unwanted child, or the unborn child who didn't ask to be aborted, depending on one's stance. "All you need is love," people say, as they speak out against what are perceived to be unfair rules and laws. "Legalism" is a nasty word in society; it suggests people care more about the rules than about each other. And, a common question in ethics is to ask whether it is better to do something out of obligation to a law, or out of love. Most people answer that it is far better to do something from love, and see acts of love as almost antithetical to law.

The difficulty with this is that what counts as love very much varies depending on what a person's point of view is. Moreover, because people tend to see love as an "emotion" and a psychological state, it is difficult to name what counts as loving behavior. So, note what internet conversations like the ones above readily display: rules are linked to enabling people to love each other better – or at least treat each other in better ways. The authors of rules for discussion forums and blogs see rules as a way of maintaining and preserving certain kinds of spaces online, spaces that form people to be and do better, for the specific purpose of being Christian. This does not mean, of course, that there are not arguments about what the most loving action looks like, but it does mean that online theological conversation more readily displays the connections between rules and virtues in ways that offline conversations do not. There are few offline spaces where people discuss good rules and what they hope to achieve by them; perhaps it is the very nature of a Web 2.0 space designed for dialogue that means rules *especially* get discussed online, though.

Another aspect of online life that can fare better in online conversation is accountability. Some may laugh at this assertion, seeing that the internet hides peoples' identities and allows them not to be accountable. This is true when it comes to individuals;

when it comes to online communal standards, however, this is less true. Even anonymous individuals cannot "troll" groups and expect not to be reprimanded or expelled from a discussion group. That is, online communities, especially online Christian communities, are practicing something similar to excommunication or shunning.

In offline contexts, many people see shunning or excommunication as strange, out of date, and incompatible with Christian love and human freedom. A key example is found in many online comments surrounding the case of a pregnant woman in Arizona. The woman was admitted to a Catholic hospital with pulmonary hypertension, a rare but often fatal condition. The doctors determined that they needed to end the pregnancy in order to save the mother's life. Later, the nun and doctors associated with making the decision were excommunicated by Bishop Thomas J. Olmsted.[33] One representative commenter at the "Abortion Gang" blog writes, "this was a bit too extreme. Excommunication? C'mon folks, we live in 2010, get over it. It's not like she performed the abortion herself or went around marching in a pro-life parade."[34] The commenter alludes to the fact that we live in 2010 as though the contemporary time period ought to mean excommunication is no longer practiced. Moreover, on the commenter's view, what the nun did is not extreme enough for the radical punishment of excommunication.

It is curious, therefore, that when online Christian communities exhibit similar kinds of practices, it is seen as a matter of justice, fairness, and integrity. Online participants rejoice when "trolls" are removed from circulation. Moderators of Christian forums have required public apologies on occasion, or otherwise required people to own up to mistakes in interactions with people. Online groups therefore may be well able to form peoples' lives in ways that many offline communities in our present modern-day context cannot do.

---

[33] Michael Clancy, "Nun at St. Joseph's Hospital Rebuked over Abortion to Save Woman," *The Arizona Republic*, (May 10, 2010) http://www.azcentral.com/arizonarepublic/news/articles/2010/05/15/20100515phoenix-catholic-nun-abortion.html. Accessed August 24, 2011.

[34] "Excommunication in the Face of Choice," *Abortion Gang*, (May 18, 2010) http://abortiongang.org/2010/05/excommunication-in-the-face-of-choice/#comments. Accessed August 24, 2011.

The good life in a technological age. . .

So, as I've tried to outline above, it may be the case that internet technology aids in practicing certain aspects of Christian life well. However, I think that each of the examples I have given above could easily have an offline counter-example. There are all kinds of ways in which Christians are not better Christians online, as the Rob Bell saga shows.

This fact once again makes my point: one of the difficulties about discussing online and offline life is that it is often impossible to make an intelligible distinction between the two. In the introductory chapter, I mentioned that some detractors of online life and conversation make their cases in terms of the internet's Gnostic, bodiless tendencies, and they contrast that with the presumed embodied aspects of offline interactions. This relates to the charge of individualism online that I've been discussing in this chapter, because peoples' idea of the internet as an individualistic enterprise presumes that there are individuals disconnected from the rest of the world, focused solely on themselves in relation to an online world. Yet I have tried to show that people can be formed for good in a variety of ways, including online.

The difficulty, I argue, is less with the specific technologies that we use and more with the societal stories that are inseparable from those technologies, but which, nonetheless, can be changed, bit by bit, to reflect a better story about what technology means for us. When it comes to ethics, it is those stories that comprise the main problem. Indeed, in a world where I can be connected online via my smart phone while yet being in the middle of a group of friends waiting to sit down in a restaurant, an online/offline distinction has very little value – yet ethics, questions about how I might live well and become the best person I can be, still remains important.

For example, one of the societal stories we tell ourselves is that society is voluntaristic. We can choose our cars, we can choose our churches, we can choose where to work. We can enter and leave communities. So, in the case of excommunication or shunning as mentioned above, how often will it be the case that someone will not hang around to apologize, but will simply choose to go elsewhere – even if learning to apologize might make someone a better human being? Human will and choice takes precedence over everything else, even when we are liable to make poor choices that do not aid in getting us where we want to be.

Of course, ours is not the first society that has noted the presence of human choice. Thomas Aquinas notes that human actions are "properly called human" (as opposed to actions that animals also do) when a human being is able to be "master" of those actions through will.[35] Thomas's understanding of human action and choice differs in at least two important ways from our contemporary view of choice. The first is that true human choice involves reason; the second is that true human choice involves recognition that a choice aims toward a purpose. Eating a fast food meal of a double-patty burger, a large order of fries, and a chocolate shake "because I want to" states a person's choice, but a statement of this kind does not make any mention of reasons, nor any awareness that eating this fast food meal might not, in fact, help a person reach the goal he or she wants to attain (e.g. lower cholesterol or lower weight).

Part of this story that privileges unfettered choice is also a story that privileges describing bad choices and evil done in terms of addiction. In a world where choice is everything and the best thing, one of the few psychologically acceptable options for saying that I made a "poor choice" is to use the language of addiction. Addiction is a term that frequently figures in discussions of online use because technological machines are so compelling. As Sherry Turkle mentions, when describing how people plug into their online social networks, but lose any desire to interact with offline people: "It is tempting, of course, to see all of this in terms of addiction. . . . The addiction metaphor fits a common experience: the more time spent online, the more one wants to spend time online."[36] The only recourse is not to use the addicting thing. As technology is one of our many contemporary addictions, so there are theologians who speak of dumping that addiction. Yet, few people truly dump their technology; technology is becoming a bit like eating. If a person sees herself as addicted to food, it is not possible to "dump" all food, for that would lead to certain death. It is likewise impossible

---

[35] *Summa Theologica* I.II. 1. 1.

[36] Sherry Turkle, *Alone Together: Why We Expect More From Technology and Less From Each Other* Kindle Edition (New York: Basic Books, 2011), locs 5602–10.

– in a world where medical records and grocery bills and votes are all recorded on computers and often online – to separate from technology. Even Christians who decide to give up the internet for Lent, as discussed in Chapter 3, usually end up taking it back up again at Easter. So Turkle goes on to say: "considering ourselves victims of a bad substance is not a good first step. . . ."[37]

The difficulty with addiction is we learn to see ourselves only in relation to the power the addiction holds over us, which leads to passivity and futility. We cannot become better people; ethics becomes impossible. Theologically, we would be better off thinking about sin, rather than addiction. Sin more aptly describes human capacity to respond to our world, rather than succumb to it. Part of the Christian theologian's task, no matter the context in which the theology is done, is to think through sinful practices and to recognize that those practices affect a person's entire character and ability to allow God to be part of one's life. This is regardless of whether those actions are done some place we call "online" or "offline."

"We have to find a way to live with seductive technology and make it work to our purposes. This is hard and will take work."[38] Such hard work is, in fact, the work of theological practical reasoning. Through examination of sin, the view of God as humanity's final end, and reflective practical reasoning – which involves healthy skepticism of both an overly joyous approach to internet culture or an overly dark condemnation of internet culture – we begin to see ways of taming the internet so that we Christians can aim for our goal, which is life in God. In the final chapter of this book, I discuss some of the practices that online and offline theologians have suggested, in order to enable this kind of practical wisdom.

---

[37] Ibid., locs. 5602–10.
[38] Ibid.

Conclusion: "The new and the old"— practicing internet theology

'The kingdom of heaven is like treasure hidden in a field, which someone found and hid; then in his joy he goes and sells all that he has and buys that field.

'Again, the kingdom of heaven is like a merchant in search of fine pearls; on finding one pearl of great value, he went and sold all that he had and bought it.

'Again, the kingdom of heaven is like a net that was thrown into the sea and caught fish of every kind; when it was full, they drew it ashore, sat down, and put the good into baskets but threw out the bad. So it will be at the end of the age. The angels will come out and separate the evil from the righteous and throw them into the furnace of fire, where there will be weeping and gnashing of teeth.

'Have you understood all this?' They answered, 'Yes.' And he said to them, 'Therefore every scribe who has been trained for the kingdom of heaven is like the master of a household who brings out of his treasure what is new and what is old.'

Matthew 13:44–52[1]

This passage from Matthew's gospel is helpful for thinking about theology on the internet because it juxtaposes what is new and old with what is good and bad, all the terms that come up frequently in discussion about theology online. Curiously, what is new is

---

[1] NRSV.

not necessarily good or bad in these parables; what is old is also not necessarily good or bad. Rather, when Jesus compares "every scribe" who knows about the Kingdom of heaven with heads of households who take from the storeroom what is new and old, he suggests that the scribes will interpret what is old via what is new. One commenter on the Bible says: "The mere scribe, Rabbinical in spirit, produces only the old and stale. The disciple of the kingdom like the Master, is always fresh-minded, yet knows how to value all old spiritual treasures of Holy Writ, or Christian tradition."[2] The traditions handed on through the Old Testament are not rejected out of hand, but reinterpreted. What is good or bad is left to the determination of God, who will direct angels to "separate the evil from the righteous" at the end of time. Household heads are not therefore charged to separate the new and the old, as though they were good and bad, but to reinterpret what is new and old in light of God's revelation.

At several points in this book, I have suggested the ways in which life is simply intermixed, online and offline both. While I think it is possible and necessary to make distinctions between being connected or disconnected to the internet, it is impossible to name discretely where those connections begin and end. The internet does do something new, somewhat, but because it is also tied to the entirety of Christian tradition, it is not wholly, distinctly new. I have therefore sought to confront theologians who seek to name the internet as new and old, good and bad. For some, the internet provides a temptation to add in the new, and jettison the old (bad) forms of Christian life. For others, the internet provides a mostly bad distraction from "older," better ways of living. I have tried to show instances of it all: good, bad, old, new, and more, but through it all demonstrating that while there may be an intelligible distinction between being "online" and not being online, there is not an intelligible difference in how Christians undertake reflecting on and living a life of Christian witness.

I have shown people carrying out uncivil conversations with each other and reinforcing objectification of other human beings through their pornographic use through slavery on Second Life, or through

---

[2] A. T. Robertson, *Word Pictures in the New Testament*, Christian Classics Ethereal Library, http://www.ccel.org/ccel/robertson_at/wp_matt.xv.html. Accessed September 27, 2011.

a desire to be connected to the internet to the detriment of physical, face-to-face interaction with family and friends. However, I keep coming back to times when internet relationships and communities have provided solace, space for forming virtues, and opportunity to become better human beings. I have seen people separated physically by thousands of miles, and who know each other only by their screen names, reach out to a grieving mother though prayer and through sending her offline care packages. I have seen people who engage in heated debates online express great desire and happiness at meeting "in person." I have been the recipient of prayer instigated online, online-inspired care packages, and friendships begun online and continued offline myself.

One of the points I have tried to make in this book is that the judgments people have tried to make about the internet do not precisely map on to the ways human interactions work. Humans grow and change; this is one of the definitions of what it means to be human. But if we are not to become captives to that growth and change, always seeking the next new thing, where the only thing that exists is progress and we question even whether we ourselves exist, there must be some good account of our continuity with the past. If we are not to become lost to ourselves, losing even our knowledge about what actions are irreconcilable with Christian life, we must have some description of how what we see as Christian life online links us with the whole of Christian life together.

Theologian Herbert McCabe claims: "A real development creates a new kind of continuity within which the old is contained as well as transcended. Every creative advance of a living thing restates the whole of its history as a new kind of unity."[3] As living creatures, many of whom now reside in a technological world and can count ourselves as social cyborgs, our task is to understand ourselves once again as God's creatures. Can we tell the story of ourselves truthfully, not only in such a way that we can clearly see what is not worthy of Christian life, but also in such a way that we can accept and own what is fruitful discipleship? This is the task that online and offline theologians have in this internet age.

How might theologians interpret what seems new in relation to what seems old, in order to be faithful to God's working in all

---

[3] Herbert McCabe, *Law, Love and Language* (London: Continuum, 2003), 23–4.

of creation? As I mentioned in the first chapter, theology is about words, but these are not mere words. Our language and way of speaking together implies that we, as Christians, have a particular kind of life together. The theology we speak about God leads to the realization that "Christian beliefs are. . .deeply implicated in the actual lives of Christian individuals, families, and communities."[4] Accordingly, I suggest what kinds of habits encourage online theologians to live that Christian life. These habits come from what internet theologians themselves have suggested, and I place them here in chapter order. This chapter only provides a beginning discussion, but one I hope might be continued and developed as we continue, as the whole people of God, to reflect on the growing, changing Power of the internet in the world.

Read in diverse ways

Despite what Susan Wise Bauer mentions about reading scripture (see Chapter 2), there is something to the argument that Mark Bauerlein makes in *The Dumbest Generation* about online "reading." Internet spaces encourage skimming; people are not learning to read in nuanced, deep ways to understand complex arguments.[5] Moreover, people are being taught to privilege multitasking, which is closely connected to this online form of reading. Given that the internet is now a primary mode of encountering information, it is no bad thing to learn to use the internet well and rightly, including learning to read web pages well, which means also that online practice needs to involve practical reasoning about making judgments about link quality or generating good Google searches.

At the same time, recent studies have also shown that "multitaskers don't perform well on any of the tasks they are attempting."[6] Here

---

[4] Dorothy C. Bass, "Introduction," in *Practicing Theology: Beliefs and Practices in Christian Life*, Miroslav Volf and Dorothy C. Bass, eds (Grand Rapids, MI: Eerdmans Publishing Company, 2002), 3.

[5] Mark Bauerlein, *The Dumbest Generation: How the Digital Age Stupefies Young Americans and Jeopardizes Our Future [Or, Don't Trust Anyone Under 30]*, (New York: Jeremy P. Tarcher/Penguin, 2008), especially Chapter 4.

[6] Sherry Turkle, *Alone Together: Why We Expect More From Technology and Less From Each Other* (New York: Basic Books, 2011). Kindle Edition. Locs. 3181–8.

is yet another point where offline Christian practice can help. The discovery that we do not read well online ought to prompt Christians to think about the many ways Christians have learned to read, especially scripture. I highlight two here.

There is, for example, the monastic habit of *lectio divina*, a way of slowly digesting scripture by reading short passages several times and meditating on them. This method of reading is about as exact an opposite as one can get from online reading, but it is a way of learning patience and waiting on God, who after all, does not necessarily act in accordance with the same time expectations that we humans do.

Modern Christians have learned to read scripture in conversation with commentaries and Bible studies. Such reading asks Christians to consider a variety of sources and perspectives and not simply accept one's own individual reading as the best way. Practicing reading in this way can help avoid the online individualistic tendencies of which I have spoken in previous chapters.

Having diverse ways of reading allows Christians to have more freedom to identify the best action in any given situation. This freedom, in turn, makes us not only more capable of resisting and taming the internet, as Power, but also more capable of having better online and offline theological conversations.

One of the best theological conversations I have been part of online was with a group of lay Catholic women, who were discussing a *Commonweal* article[7] on abortion. This conversation came in the aftermath of a bishop's decision to excommunicate several people in relation to abortion done when a woman's life had been seriously endangered, along with her unborn child's. One woman linked the *Commonweal* article that spoke against the bishop's decision; several women read it. The article made the women seek out primary sources online and read them, to see the broader context. As they did reading and investigating, they shared their experiences with abortion and their thoughts about women's lives being endangered. The conversation went to very close readings of many texts, and to people wanting to make careful distinctions about what they were

---

[7] Therese Lysaught, "Moral Analysis of an Intervention Performed at St. Joseph's Hospital and Medical Center," *Commonweal Magazine* blog, (December 2010) http://www.commonwealmagazine.org/blog/wp-content/uploads/2010/12/St.-Josephs-Hospital-Analysis.pdf. Accessed January 2, 2011.

saying. This could not have happened, though, had these women not learned to read in a variety of ways.[8]

Practice imagination

Imagine the human being at the other "end" of the wire. Also imagine better ways to engage with human beings offline. Do not allow technology to make human beings into its own image (as happened in an example Turkle gives from one of her studies: "I'll pull up my friend. . .uh, my phone.")[9] Objectification of others is one of the many dangers that plagues social cyborgs, as I discuss in Chapter 3.

Practicing this kind of imagination requires, in the first place, some account of what it means to be human, and that necessarily means not solely engaging with people as objects. On this point, Wendell Berry writes:

> It is well understood that technological innovation always requires the discarding of the 'old model' – the 'old model' in this case being not just our old Royal standard, but my wife, my critic, my closest reader, my fellow worker. Thus (and I think this is typical of present-day technological innovation), what would be superseded would be not only something but somebody. In order to be technologically up-to-date as a writer, I would have to sacrifice an association that I am dependent upon and that I treasure.[10]

Berry's argument is that people become supplanted by this desire for new things, which in turn gives evidence of what we really like: sleek, fast, efficient machines with cool graphics. People's companionship pales by comparison. Two decades after Berry's essay, Sherry Turkle finds evidence for just such a thing occurring

---

[8] http://forums.delphiforums.com/nfptalk/messages?msg=140830.1. Accessed January 2, 2011.

[9] Turkle, loc. 3413.

[10] Wendell Berry, "Why I am Not Going to Buy a Computer," in *What Are People For?* (New York: North Point Press, 1990), 171.

in her book *Alone Together*, in which she worries that technology prevents us from being able even to identify other human beings, because they become objects.[11]

Developing good offline relationships is key to the health of online relationships, as I think Richard Beck showed in his research on his students and their Facebook habits (from Chapter 5), where he suggests that they use Facebook to enhance existing relationships.[12] People do develop relationships with otherwise complete strangers online, but these are exceptions to the rule; by developing already existing offline relationships, online, people thereby develop enough of a comfort level in order to friend strangers.

So then, the question becomes how to develop human relationships, or put in more theological terms, how to love one's neighbor. Jesus gave many possible answers to this question, among them: to treat others as Christ himself.[13] That becomes the source and substance of developing this new imagination.

Turn off, purposefully

Through the course of writing this book, I was struck many times by how often people mention both feeling seduced by the screen or addicted to their online life, and also by how often they said that the remedy was to turn off, at set periods of time. This was not a specifically Christian impulse: I was rather astounded, for example, to read the following quote from Eric Schmidt, CEO of Google. com: "You're actually going to have to turn off your phone and discover all that is happening around us. Nothing beats holding the hand of your grandchild as he walks his first steps."[14] "Turning off" is wisdom many internet users have shared, though, because they have recognized how easy it is to be engulfed by the internet and have it become the main, if not the only means of identification.

---

[11] Turkle, Loc. 3299.

[12] Richard Beck, "How Facebook Killed the Church," at http://experimentaltheology. blogspot.com/2010/03/how-facebook-killed-church.html. Accessed March 20, 2011.

[13] Matthew 25: 31–46.

[14] Cited in William Powers, *Hamlet's Blackberry: A Practical Philosophy for Building a Good Life in the Digital Age* (New York: Harper Collins, 2010), 76.

Most of the online theologians I have mentioned in this book turn off at one point or another. In Chapter 3, I showed some of the conversations about "turning off" as a Lenten practice. It might also be linked to a practice of the Sabbath. Abraham Joshua Heschel, whose writing on the Sabbath has been highly influential for Jews and Christians, notes:

> Six days a week we live under the tyranny of things of space; on the Sabbath we try to become attuned to holiness in time. It is a day on which we are called upon to share in what is eternal in time, to turn from the results of creation to the mystery of creation; from the world of creation to the creation of the world.[15]

It is not, for Heschel, that observing the Sabbath means withdrawing from creation, but that observing the Sabbath means seeing the world rightly. Creation is tyrannical – just as the internet as creature and Power is tyrannical – when we fail to know that we, and the world both, are creatures, as I mention in Chapter 4. Knowing this then, we return to the spaces where we inevitably live and work, but with a better view.

Be part of Christian community, online and offline

I have seen people say that their online communities are where they find "true" Christian community and support; indeed, this is the latent assumption in some of the books about internet churches that I mention in Chapter 5. What I hope this book has shown, however, is that online community cannot be neatly cornered away from offline life, though conceptually that is what we try to do sometimes.

If one is bothering to do theology on the internet (for I think there is not *yet* the necessity of being online to do theology), recognize that there is danger in assuming that one's "true" Christian community

---

[15] Abraham Joshua Heschel, *The Sabbath* (New York: Farrar, Straus, and Giroux, 1975), x.

can only be found online (or offline). Search engines, with their selective search processes, the difficulty of encountering the "other" online, and the rise of special advocacy groups (as I show in Chapter 4), suggest an inherent idolatry in wishing for Christian community to be solely online. Additionally, the internet caters to practicing some virtues but not others (such as patience), and whatever virtues may be learned online always also stand the chance of becoming vices.

Vice happens offline too, just as idolatry does. I have shown also some of the ways that online theologians make statements worth saying to Christians. The advantage offline Christian communities have, however, is long-established practices that have enabled Christians to live more virtuously, as well as a broader array of Christian practices. There are quite simply practices that humans cannot do online: fasting, even by avatar, might be a case in point. Yet the fullness of Christian life should not be arbitrarily truncated in favor of the mode of community.

Practice stability in community

In both online and offline communities it is, interestingly, stability in community that aids in better thought and conversation, as hard as that is. The rules of various communities (as I discuss in Chapter 6) form people in particular ways; these rules operate best in the presence of stability. There is a reason why, when Saint Benedict lists all the "instruments of good works" that comprise Christian life such as reading scripture, praying, not being angry or vengeful, and so on, he suggests that this must be done in "stability in the community."[16] Practicing Christian life is difficult enough in community, and nearly impossible alone, which is one of the reasons why Benedict is discouraging of monks who live alone or in twos or threes, but without any kind of rule.[17] Stability encourages a person to remain long enough to receive encouragement in Christian practices.

---

[16] Benedict, *The Rule of Saint Benedict* (Collegeville, MN: The Liturgical Press, 1981), Chapter 4.

[17] Benedict, Chapter 1.

If a person hangs around particular communities found in forums, blogs, and so on, one does, actually, begin to encounter the kinds of diversity that Google searches will not give, even online. It is in stability that one begins to encounter tough conversations with others, even in special advocacy groups, exactly because it is in stability that we learn that we are all humans and we change.

Stability is not often valued in culture: theologians decry a church-shopping mentality and a "cafeteria-style" approach to morality. And yet, online and offline, we still respect stability and it is still a path toward goodness. It is the blogs that have been around the longest that have the most respect; the blog commenters who have hung around for a while whose words generally garner more respect than those commenters who make a fly-by, sweeping statement; the trolls who are dismissed in favor of people who take the time to remain with others. A dedication to stability enhances ability to be part of theological conversations in more and better ways.

Conclusion

It is no mistake that these habits show up strongly online as well as in Christian traditions down through the centuries. It is also the case that these disciplines and others not named here might develop in other ways, over time and via practical wisdom of internet practitioners. What is apparently "old" is not old so much as it is deemed worthwhile for Christian disciples, even in new technological contexts. We stewards of Christian theology and witness in this "new" internet age are responsible for sifting through the new and the old, most especially to keep what is of value.

Aquinas is on the web, or at least his successors are, and so is much else of value for good and faithful Christian witness in an internet age. May we do theology online in ways that live up to our vocation as Christians.

BIBLIOGRAPHY

Adam, AKMA. *Disseminary: Wisdom Wants to Be Free*. http://
disseminary.org., 2003.

[Author unknown.] "Dr. Peter Slade to Present Lecture Series." *Covenant
College: In All Things Christ Preeminent*. January 26, 2011. http://
www.covenant.edu/news/01.26.11_2. Accessed September 23, 2011.

Bailenson, Jeremy N. et al. "Facial Similarity Between Voters and
Candidates Causes Influence." *Public Opinion Quarterly* 72.5. http://
poq.oxfordjournals.org/content/72/5/935.full. Accessed April 12, 2011.

Bailey, Justin A. "Welcome to the Blogosphere." In *Everyday Theology:
How to Read Cultural Texts and Interpret Trends*. Kevin Vanhoozer,
ed. Grand Rapids, MI: Baker Academic Press, 2007, 173–90.

Barbour, Ian G. *Nature, Human Nature and God*. Minneapolis, MN:
Fortress Press, 2002.

Bass, Dorothy C. "Introduction." In *Practicing Theology: Beliefs and
Practices in Christian Life*. Miroslav Volf and Dorothy C. Bass, eds.
Grand Rapids, MI: Eerdmans Publishing Company, 2002.

Bauer, Susan W. "Disappearing Words: Part I: The Bad News." *The Well-
Trained Mind: Classical Education for the Next Generation*. May
5, 2011. http://www.welltrainedmind.com/reflections-on-education/
disappearing-words-part-i-the-bad-news. Accessed June 30, 2008.

_____. "Disappearing Words, Part II: What Exactly Are We Worried
About?" *The Well-Trained Mind: Classical Education for the
Next Generation*. May 6, 2011. http://www.welltrainedmind.com/
reflections-on-education/disappearing-words-part-ii-what-exactly-are-
we-worried-about/. Accessed June 30, 2011.

_____. "Disappearing Words, III. Wrong Assumptions." *The Well-
Trained Mind: Classical Education for the Next Generation*. May
8, 2011. http://www.welltrainedmind.com/reflections-on-education/
disappearing-words-part-ii-what-exactly-are-we-worried-about.
Accessed June 30, 2008.

_____. "Disappearing Words, Part IV: What do we do about it?" *The
Well-Trained Mind: Classical Education for the Next Generation*.
May 11, 2011. http://www.welltrainedmind.com/reflections-on-

education/disappearing-words-part-iv-what-do-we-do-about-it.
Accessed June 13, 2011.

Bauerlein, Mark. *The Dumbest Generation: How the Digital Age
Stupefies Young Americans and Jeopardizes Our Future [Or, Don't
Trust Anyone Under 30].* New York: Jeremy P. Tarcher/Penguin, 2008.

Bazin, Jean N., and Jérôme Cottin. *Virtual Christianity: Potential and
Challenge for the Churches.* Geneva: WCC Publications, 2004.

Bball1989. "Rob Bell – Love Wins (Remake: Jesus Wins)." *YouTube.*
April 19, 2011. http://www.youtube.com/watch?v=pDLCN8GwBHE.
Accessed July 14, 2011.

Beck, Fr. Edward L. "Confession App: Catholic Church Sanctions New
iPhone App." *ABC News Online.* February 8, 2011. Online: http://
abcnews.go.com/Technology/confession-app-roman-catholic-church-
sanctions-iphone-app/story?id=12866499. Accessed February 8,
2011.

Beck, Richard. "How Facebook Killed the Church." *Experimental
Theology: The Thoughts, Articles, and Essays of Richard Beck.* March
5, 2010. http://experimentaltheology.blogspot.com/2010/03/how-
facebook-killed-church.html.

Bednar, Tim. "We Know More than Our Pastors: Why Bloggers are
the Vanguard of the Participatory Church." http://www.scribd.com/
doc/47331/We-Know-More-Than-Our-Pastors.

Belcher, Kimberly H. "Tweeting the Summa Theologiae." *PrayTell Blog.*
July 13, 2010. http://www.praytellblog.com/index.php/2010/07/13/
tweeting-the-summa-theologiae.

Benedict, Saint. *The Rule of Saint Benedict.* Collegeville, MN: The
Liturgical Press, 1981.

Berry, Wendell. "Why I am Not Going to Buy a Computer." In *What Are
People For?.* New York: North Point Press, 1990.

Bonhoeffer, Dietrich. *Life Together.* New York: Harper & Row
Publishers, 1954.

Borgmann, Albert. *Power Failure: Christianity in the Culture of
Technology.* Chicago, IL: Brazos Press, 2003.

_____. *Technology and the Character of Contemporary Life.* Chicago, IL:
University of Chicago Press, 1987.

boyd, danah. "White Flight in Networked Publics? How Race and Class
Shaped American Teen Engagement with MySpace and Facebook." In
Race After the Internet. Lisa Nakamura and Peter Chow-White, eds.
New York: Routledge, 2011: 203–22.

Briggs, Brian. "Browser Showdown: Firefox vs. Internet Explorer."
BBspot. http://www.bbspot.com/News/2005/01/firefox_vs_internet_
explorer.html. Accessed June 1, 2006.

Brock, Brian. *Christian Ethics in a Technological Age.* Grand Rapids, MI:
Eerdmans, 2010.

Brookey, Robert A. "Paradise Crashed: Rethinking MMORPGs and Other Virtual Worlds, An Introduction." *Critical Studies in Media Communications*. 26.2 (2009): 101–3.

Brookey, Robert A., and Kristopher L. Cannon. "Sex Lives in Second Life." *Critical Studies in Media Communication*. 26.2 (2009): 154–64.

Brooks, David. "The Messiah Complex." *The New York Times Online*. January 7, 2010. http://www.nytimes.com/2010/01/08/opinion/08brooks.html?ref=opinion. Accessed June 3, 2011.

Butler, Judith. *Bodies that Matter: On the Discursive Limits of Sex*. New York: Routledge Press, 1993.

_____. *Gender Trouble*. New York: Routledge Press, 1990.

Butt, Riazat. "Pope Claims Condoms Could Make AIDS Crisis Worse." *The Guardian*. March 17, 2009. Online: http://www.guardian.co.uk/world/2009/mar/17/pope-africa-condoms-aids. Accessed December 21, 2009.

Campbell, Heidi. *Exploring Religious Community Online: We Are One in the Network*. New York: Peter Lang, 2005.

Carter, J. Kameron. "Avatar: An Amazing and Troubling Film." *J. Kameron Carter*. (March 12, 2010). http://jkameroncarter.com/?p=56. Accessed June 3, 2011.

_____. *Race: A Theological Account*. New York: Oxford UP, 2008.

Cherney, James. "Deaf Culture and the Cochlear Implant Debate: Cyborg Politics and the Identity of People with Disabilities." *Argumentation and Advocacy* 36.1 (Summer 1999): 22–34.

Chuang, D. J. "Why Churches Must Innovate or Die." *Learnings @ Leadership Network*. April 27, 2009. http://learnings.leadnet.org/2009/04/why-churches-must-innovate.html. Accessed February 23, 2011.

Clancy, Michael. "Nun at St. Joseph's Hospital Rebuked over Abortion to Save Woman." *The Arizona Republic* (May 10, 2010). http://www.azcentral.com/arizonarepublic/news/articles/2010/05/15/20100515pho enix-catholic-nun-abortion.html. Accessed August 24, 2011.

Cobb, Jennifer. "Can We Love the Stranger on Facebook." *Being Blog*. April 7, 2011. Krista Tippett, blog owner. American Public Media. http://blog.onbeing.org/post/4413019671/can-we-love-the-stranger-on-facebook. Accessed May 26, 2011.

Cole, Helena and Mark Griffiths. "Social Interactions in Massively Multiplayer Online Role-Playing Gamers." *CyberPsychology and Behavior*. 10.4 (2007): 575–83.

Compier, Don. *What is Rhetorical Theology? Textual Practice and Public Discourse*. Harrisburg, PA: Trinity International Press, 1999.

Cunningham, David S. *Faithful Persuasion: In Aid of a Rhetoric of Christian Theology*. Notre Dame; London: University of Notre Dame Press, 1990.

Dawn, Marva. *Powers, Weakness and the Tabernacling of God.* Grand Rapids, MI: Eerdmans, 2001. Kindle Edition.

Dayton, Andy. "The Rapture of the Geeks." *Being Blog.* Krista Tippett, blog owner. American Public Media. http://blog.onbeing.org/post/37176264/the-rapture-of-the-geeks-andy-dayton-associate. Accessed May 26, 2011.

Den, Frank. "Introduction." *The Internet is God.* November 25, 2008. http://www.theinternetisgod.org/book/internet-god/introduction. Accessed March 1, 2011.

DenverSeoMarketing.com. "Determining Link Value and Relative Value." http://www.denverseomarketing.com/Link-Hierarchy.htm. Accessed September 19, 2011.

Desiree. "Is Studying Christian Theology Flawed Because the Entire Subject Rests on the Belief that Myths are True?" *Yahoo Answers.* 2010. http://answers.yahoo.com/question/index;_ylt=At3puprUGp9Puvqua85XQO AjzKIX;_ylv=3?qid=20100422211906AAv9TOJ. Accessed September 2, 2011.

DeWolf, Elsie. *The House in Good Taste.* New York: 1913. Cited in Adrian Rorty, *Objects of Desire: Design and Society 1750–1980.* London: Cameron Books, 1986.

Douthat, Ross. "Heaven and Nature." *The New York Times* online. December 20, 2009. http://www.nytimes.com/2009/12/21/opinion/21douthat1.html. Accessed April 18, 2011.

Drescher, Elizabeth. "Digital Dust-Up: Lenten Practice in the Digital Reformation." *Elizabeth Drescher, PhD.* March 19, 2011. http://www.elizabethdrescher.net/ElizabethdrescherNet/My_Blog/Entries/2011/3/19_Digital_Dust-Up__Lenten_Practice_in_the_Digital_Reformation.html. Accessed May 16, 2011.

_____. "Facebook Doesn't Kill Churches, Churches Kill Churches." *Religious Dispatches Magazine* online. March 16, 2011. http://www.religiondispatches.org/archive/atheologies/4390/facebook_doesn%27t_kill_churches%2C_churches_kill_churches. Accessed 20 March 2011.

_____. *Tweet if you [Heart] Jesus: Practicing Church in the Digital Reformation.* New York: Morehouse Publishing, 2011.

Dyer, John. "Not Many of You Should Presume to Be Bloggers." *Christianity Today* online. March 3, 2011. http://www.christianitytoday.com/ct/2011/marchweb-only/bloggers.html. Accessed August 22, 2011.

Eckholm, Eric. "Pastor Stirs Wrath with his Views on Old Questions." *New York Times* online. March 4, 2011. http://www.nytimes.com/2011/03/05/us/05bell.html. Accessed August 22, 2011.

Eisenstein, Elizabeth. *The Printing Press as an Agent of Change.* 2 vols. Cambridge: Cambridge UP, 1980.

Elliot, Carl. *Better Than Well: American Medicine Meets the American Dream.* New York: W.W. Norton & Company, 2003.

Estes, Douglas. *SimChurch: Being the Church in the Virtual World.* Grand Rapids, MI: Zondervan, 2009.

Evans, Rachel H. "A Christian's Guide to Not Being A Jerk on the Internet." *Rachel Held Evans Author Speaker Blogger.* May 4, 2011. http://rachelheldevans.com/christian-guide-internet. Accessed July 18, 2011.

"Excommunication in the Face of Choice." *Abortion Gang.* May 18, 2010. http://abortiongang.org/2010/05/excommunication-in-the-face-of-choice/#comments. August 24, 2011.

Fiddes, Paul "Sacraments in a Virutal World?" *Brownblog.* June 22, 2009. http://brownblog.info/?p=886.

Foss, Elizabeth. "An Internet Fast for Lent?" *Arlington Catholic Herald.* February 24, 2010. http://www.catholicherald.com/opinions/detail. html?sub_id=12424. Accessed May 17, 2011.

FRCInternet. "Flamingo Road Church First Internet Baptism." *YouTube.* March 22, 2008. http://www.youtube.com/watch?v=qThUe1-RvXU. Accessed February, 2011.

Friesen, Dwight. *Thy Kingdom Connected: What the Church Can Learn from Facebook, the Internet, and Other Networks.* Chicago, IL: Baker Books, 2009.

Frugal Trenches. "On Lent and Things." *Notes from the Frugal Trenches – A Downshifting Journey.* March 8, 2011. http://notesfromthefrugaltrenches.com/2011/03/08/on-lent-and-things/. Accessed May 17, 2011.

———. "Reclaiming Simple Sundays." *Notes from the Frugal Trenches – A Downshifting Journey.* March 13, 2011. http://notesfromthefrugaltrenches.com/2011/03/13/reclaiming-simple-sundays-20. Accessed May 17, 2011.

"A Gay Girl in Damascus." *AlJazeera* online. June 13, 2011. http://english.aljazeera.net/news/middleeast/2011/06/2011671229558865.html. Accessed June 15, 2011.

Godzieba, Anthony. "Quaestio Disputata: The Magisterium in an Age of Digital Reproduction." In *When the Magisterium Intervenes.* Collegeville: The Liturgical Press, forthcoming 2012.

Grigoriadis, Vanessa. "Do You Own Facebook or Does Facebook Own You?" *New York Times Magazine* (April 5, 2009). Online: http://nymag.com/news/features/55878. Accessed April 19, 2011.

Haraway, Donna. "A Cyborg Manifesto: Science, Technology, and Socialist-Feminism in the Late Twentieth Century." In *Simians, Cyborgs and Women: The Reinvention of Nature.* New York; Routledge Press, 1991: 149–81.

Hart, David B. *The Beauty of the Infinite: The Aesthetics of Christian Truth*. Grand Rapids, MI: Eerdmans, 2003.

Hauerwas, Stanley. *A Community of Character:Toward a Constructive Christian Social Ethic*. Notre Dame, IN: University of Notre Dame Press, 1981.

____. "A Story-Formed Community: Reflections on *Watership Down*." In *The Hauerwas Reader*. John Berkman and Michael Cartwright. Eds. Durham, NC: Duke University Press, 2001.

Heever, James van den. "Web 2.0: Technology for the Postmodern Sensibility and its Implications for the Church." *Journal of Theology for Southern Africa* 132 (2008): 86–107.

Heschel, Abraham J. *The Sabbath*. New York: Farrar, Straus, and Giroux, 1975.

Hess, Mary E. "Pedagogy and Theology in Cyberspace." *Teaching Theology and Religion* 5.1 (2002): 30–8.

Himanen, Pekka. *The Hacker Ethic and the Spirit of the Information Age*. New York: Random House, 2001.

Hipps, Shane. *Flickering Pixels: How Technology Shapes Your Faith*. Grand Rapids, MI: Zondervan, 2009.

Hussain, Zaheer and Mark Griffiths, "Gender Swapping and Socializing in Cyberspace: An Exploratory Study." *CyberPsychology and Behavior* 11.1 (2008): 47–53.

Hwang, Tim. "Wikileaks and the Internet's Long War." *Washington Post* online (December 12, 2010). http://www.washingtonpost.com/wp-dyn/content/article/2010/12/10/AR2010121002604.html. Accessed February 24, 2011.

"Interview with Hubert L. Dreyfus." *Conversations with History; Institute of International Studies*. UC Berkeley (2005). http://globetrotter.berkeley.edu/people5/Dreyfus/dreyfus-con7.html. Accessed April 12, 2011.

"Japan Lab Develops Remote Kissing Device." *GMA Online*. May 3, 2011. http://www.gmanews.tv/story/219493/technology/japan-lab-develops-remote-kissing-device. Accessed July 7, 2011.

Jennings, Willie J. *The Christian Imagination: Theology and the Origins of Race*. Hartford, CT: Yale University Press, 2011.

John of Damascus, Saint. *On the Divine Images: Three Apologies Against Those Who Attack the Divine Images*. Crestwood, NY: St Vladimir's Seminary Press, 1997.

Kallenberg, Brad. *God and Gadgets: Following Jesus in a Technological Age*. Eugene, OR: Cascade, 2011.

Kavanaugh, Andrea L. and Scott J. Patterson. "The Impact of Community Computer Networks on Social Capital and Community Involvement in Blacksburg." In *The Internet in Everyday Life*. Barry Wellman and Caroline A. Haythornthwaite, eds. Oxford: Blackwell, 2002: 325–44.

Kelsey, David. "Spiritual Machines, Personal Bodies, and God: Theological Education and Theological Anthropology." *Teaching Theology and Religion* 5.1 (2002): 2–9.

Locke, Neal. "Virtual World Churches and The Reformed Confessions." *Princeton Theological Review* XVII.2 (Fall 2010): 55–66.

Lombard, Christo J. S. "Some Ethical Dimensions to Teaching Theology via the Internet." *Journal of Theology for Southern Africa*. 115.01 (2003): 43–61.

"Love Wins." *The Work of Rob Bell* website. Video online. https://www.robbell.com/lovewins. Accessed July 14, 2011.

Lysaught, M. Therese. "Moral Analysis of an Intervention Performed at St. Joseph's Hospital and Medical Center." *Commonweal Magazine* blog (December 2010). http://www.commonwealmagazine.org/blog/wp-content/uploads/2010/12/St.-Josephs-Hospital-Analysis.pdf. Accessed January 3, 2011.

MacIntyre, Alasdair. *Whose Justice? Which Rationality?* Notre Dame, IN: University of Notre Dame Press, 1988.

Maritain, Jacques. *Art and Scholasticism, With Other Essays*. J. F. Scanlan, trans. New York: Chalres Scribner's Sons, 1930.

Maushart, Susan. *The Winter of Our Disconnect: How Three Totally Wired Teenagers (and a Mother Who Slept with Her iPhone) Pulled the Plug on their Technology and Lived to Tell the Tale*. New York: Jeremy P. Tarcher/Penguin, 2010.

McCabe, Herbert. *God Matters*. London: Mowbray, 1987.

_____. *Law, Love and Language*. London: Continuum, 2003.

McCracken, Brett. *Hipster Christianity: When Church and Cool Collide*. Chicago, IL: Baker Books, 2010.

_____. "The Separation of Church and Status: How Online Social Networking Helps and Hurts the Church." *Princeton Theological Review* XVII.2 (Fall 2010): 21–34.

McCutcheon, Russell. *The Insider/Outsider Problem in the Study of Religion: A Reader*. London: Cassell, 1999.

McGonigal, Jane. *Reality is Broken: Why Games Make Us Better and How They Can Change the World*. New York: The Penguin Press, 2011.

McLuhan, Marshall. *The Gutenberg Galaxy*. Toronto: University of Toronto Press, 1962.

Mehta, Hermant. "Ask an Atheist… (Hemant Reponds)." *Rachel Held Evans: Author, Speaker, Blogger*. July 5, 2011. http://rachelheldevans.com/ask-an-atheist-response. Accessed July 5, 2011.

Mele, Morra A. "Exploring the Gendered Web." *Gender and Technology: Berkman Center for Internet and Society*. April 17, 2009. http://blogs.law.harvard.edu/genderandtech/tag/facebook. Accessed April 19, 2011.

Miller, Vincent J. "When Mediating Structure Change: Transformations of Magisterial Authority in Digital Culture." In *When the Magisterium Intervenes*. Collegeville: Liturgical Press, forthcoming 2012).

Milton, Michael. "Acknowledge the Sin, Accentuate the Grace, Honor the Fathers: Why I Love the PCA and RTS." *Reformed Theological Seminary* website. Date unknown. http://michaelmilton.org/2010/07/09/acknowledge-the-sin-accentuate-the-grace-honor-the-fathers-why-i-love-the-pca-and-rts/. Accessed September 23, 2011.

Mitchell, Nathan. "Ritual and New Media." In *Cyberspace-Cyberethics-Cybertheology*, Erik Borgman, Stephan van Erp and Hille Haker, eds. London: SCM Press, 2005.

Nakamura, Lisa. "Don't Hate the Player, Hate the Game: The Racialization of Labor in World of Warcraft." *Critical Studies in Media Communication* 26.2 (2009): 128–44.

NowForTruth. "Gay Syrian Female Blogger Hoax." *YouTube*. June 13, 2011. http://www.youtube.com/watch?v=o_TTKfAZBfw. Accessed June 15, 2011.

Ogas, Ogi, and Sai Gaddam. *A Billion Wicked Thoughts*. New York: Penguin, 2011.

"Open Source Technology." University of Dayton Technology Conference (2009). Unpublished conference presentation.

Papacharrizzi, Zizi. "Democracy Online" *New Media and Society*. *New Media and Society* 6.2: 259–83. Online at http://www.ict-21.ch/com-ict/IMG/pdf/DemocracyOnline.pdf.

Pariser, Eli. "Ten Ways to Pop Your Filter Bubble." *The Filter Bubble*. Date unknown. http://www.thefilterbubble.com/10-things-you-can-do. Accessed July 19, 2011.

Pickell, Travis. "'Thou Has Given Me a Body': Theological Anthropology and the Virtual Church." *Princeton Theological Review* XVII.2 (Fall 2010): 67–80.

Pinches, Charles. "Hauerwas and Political Theology: The Next Generation." *Journal of Religious Ethics* 36.3 (2008): 513–42.

Pontifical Council for Social Communications. "Ethics in Internet." February 22, 2002. http://www.vatican.va/roman_curia/pontifical_councils/pccs/documents/rc_pc_pccs_doc_20020228_ethics-internet_en.html. Accessed October 20, 2010.

Powers, William. *Hamlet's Blackberry: A Practical Philosophy for Building A Good Life in the Digital Age*. New York: Harper Collins, 2010.

PrayerWorksInt. "Mass: We Pray The Video Game." *YouTube*. November 13, 2009. http://www.youtube.com/watch?v=nRMiRFJzIKA. Accessed September 15, 2011.

Ray, Audacia. *Naked on the Internet: Hookups, Downloads, and Chasing in on Internet Exploitation*. Emeryville, CA: Seal Press, 2007.

Rice, Jesse. *The Church of Facebook: How the Hyperconnected are Redefining Community.* Colorado Springs, CO: David C. Cook, 2009.

Robertson, A. T. *Word Pictures in the New Testament.* Available online at Christian Classics Ethereal Library. Broadman Press, 1932. http://www.ccel.org/ccel/robertson_at/wp_matt.xv.html.

Robertson, Margaret. "One More Go: Why *Halo* Makes Me Want to Lay Down and Die." *Offworld.* September 25, 2009. http://www.offworld.com/2009/09/one-more-go-why-halo-makes-me.html.

Rose, Devin. "Ask a Catholic....(Devin Responds)." *Rachel Held Evans Author Speaker Blogger.* July 12, 2011. http://rachelheldevans.com/ask-a-catholic-response. Accessed July 12, 2011.

Rowse, Darren. "How to Build Blog Authority." *ProBlogger.* November 8, 2006. http://www.problogger.net/archives/2006/11/08/how-to-build-blog-authority-technorati-style. Accessed January 4, 2010.

Saddington, John. "World First? Internet Baptism at Flamingo Church." *ChurchMag* September 14, 2009. http://churchm.ag/world-first-internet-baptism-by-flamingo-road. Accessed September 16, 2011.

Silk, Mark. "Avatar's Christian theme." *Spiritual Politics: A Blog on Religion and American Political Culture.* December 25, 2009. Accessed April 18, 2011. http://www.spiritual-politics.org/2009/12/avatars_christian_theme.html.

Slade, Peter. "Another Weird Idea." Podcast online. February 1, 2011. http://www.covenant.edu/node/3785.

_____. *Open Friendship in a Closed Society: Mission Mississippi and a Theology of Friendship.* New York: Oxford University Press, 2009.

Spellman, Ched. "The Canon After Google: Implications of a Digitized and Destabilized Codex." *Princeton Theological Review* XVII.2 (Fall 2010): 39–42.

Stratton, Gary D. "Danger! Angry Blogger: The Apostle Paul's Cyber-relationship Checklist." *Two Handed Warriors: Reimagining Faith and Culture One Story at a Time.* Date unknown. http://www.garydavidstratton.com/2011/faith-2/cyberspace-wins-an-update-on-the-rob-bell-controversy. Accessed August 22, 2011.

Stringfellow, William. *An Ethic for Christians and Other Aliens in a Strange Land.* Eugene, OR: Wipf and Stock, 2004.

_____. "Traits of the Principalities." In *A Keeper of the Word: Selected Writings of William Stringfellow.* Bill Wylie Kellerman, ed. Grand Rapids, MI: Eerdmans Publishing Company, 1994: 204–13.

Tamie. "ah, the church." *the Owls and the Angels.* http://owlrainfeathers.blogspot.com/2010/11/ah-church.html. Accessed March 10, 2011.

Taylor, Justin. "Rob Bell, Universalist?" *The Gospel Coalition.* February 26, 2011. http://thegospelcoalition.org/blogs/justintaylor/2011/02/26/rob-bell-universalist. Accessed August 12, 2011.

Terdman, Daniel. "Study: Wikipedia as Accurate as Britannica." *CNET News*. December 15, 2005. http://news.cnet.com/2100-1038_3-5997332.html. Accessed September 6, 2011.

"The Average Age of Facebook Users Rise," AfterMarketer Club. March 3, 2011. http://aftermarketerclub.com/blog/2011/03/the-average-age-of-facebook-users-rise. Accessed August 26, 2011.

Thomas Aquinas, Saint. *Summa Theologica*. 5 vols. Revised ed. Christian Classics, 1997.

Thomas Aquinas @ Summa Theologiae: Tweeting One Article a Day for Your Amusement and Edification. September 11, 2010. http://twitter.com/#%21/summatheologiae. Accessed June 15, 2011.

Tierney, John. "3D Avatars Could Put You in Two Places at Once." *New York Times* online. April 11, 2011. http://www.nytimes.com/2011/04/12/science/12tier.html?_r=2&nl=todaysheadlines&emc=tha26. Accessed April 11, 2011.

Turkle, Sherry. *Alone Together: Why We Expect More From Technology and Less From Each Other*. New York: Basic Books, 2011. Kindle Edition.

_____. *Life on the Screen: Identity in the Age of the Internet*. New York: Simon and Schuster, 1997.

United States Conference of Catholic Bishops. "Your Family and Cyberspace: A Statement of the US Catholic Bishops." Washington, DC: United States Catholic Conference, 2000.

Walls, Andrew. *The Missionary Movement in Christian History: Studies in Transmission of the Faith*. Maryknoll, NY: Orbis Books, 2000.

Ward, Graham. *Cities of God*. London: Routledge Press, 2001.

_____. "Between Virtue and Virtuality." *Theology Today* 59.1 (April 2002): 55–70.

"Web 2.0." http://en.wikipedia.org/wiki/Web_2.0. Accessed May 17, 2011.

Weeks, Linton. "We Are Just Not Digging the Whole Anymore." *NPR* online. March 15, 2011. http://www.npr.org/2011/03/15/134531653/we-are-just-not-digging-the-whole-anymore.

Wink, Walter. *The Powers that Be: Theology for a New Millennium*. New York: Three Rivers Press, 1999.

_____. *Unmasking the Powers: The Invisible Forces that Determine Human Existence*. Philadelphia, PA: Fortress Press, 1986.

Winner, Langdon. *The Whale and the Reactor: A Search for Limits in an Age of High Technology*. Chicago, IL: University of Chicago Press, 1986.

Yoder, John H. *The Politics of Jesus*. Second Edition. Grand Rapids, MI: Eerdmans Publishing Company, 1994.

INDEX